T0246476

A Cold Eye: Notes from a Shared Island 1989–2024

For Gerry and Dorothea, dearest of friends. CG
For Aisling and Lucas. DB

A Cold Eye: Notes from a Shared Island 1989–2024

Carlo Gébler
with photographs by David Barker

NEW ISLAND

A COLD EYE
First published in 2024 by
New Island Books
Glenshesk House
10 Richview Office Park
Clonskeagh
Dublin D14 V8C4
Republic of Ireland
www.newisland.ie

Print ISBN: 978-1-84840-900-2
eBook ISBN: 978-1-84840-901-9

British Library Cataloguing in Publication Data. A CIP catalogue record for this book is available from the British Library.

Typeset by JVR Creative India
Cover design by Mariel Deegan
Printed by L&C Printing Group, Poland, lcprinting.eu

The paper used in this book comes from the wood pulp of sustainably managed forests.

LOTTERY FUNDED

Gratefully supported by the Arts Council of Northern Ireland.

New Island Books is a member of Publishing Ireland.

10 9 8 7 6 5 4 3 2 1

Draw rein, draw breath.
Cast a cold eye
On life, on death.
Horseman pass by.
W. B. Yeats

I had seen birth and death,
But had thought they were different
Journey of the Magi, T. S. Eliot

Contents

Prologue

In 1989 a publisher commissioned me to write a book about the Troubles, as Northern Ireland's miseries were glossed. Belfast and Derry had already been exhaustively written about. The subject of my book was to be Fermanagh, because I particularly wanted to write about its border with the Republic of Ireland, where it was said that Protestants, especially those who were members of the security forces, were being ethnically cleansed by armed republicans. I also wanted to write about the bombing by the IRA of the cenotaph in Fermanagh's principal town, Enniskillen, on Remembrance Sunday 1987. The bombing had killed eleven people and injured sixty-three, many elderly. An own goal for the republican movement, which was usually so canny when it came to public relations, 'the Poppy Day bombing', as the tabloids dubbed it, had been universally criticised. The book I wrote, *The Glass Curtain: Inside an Ulster Community*, was published in 1991.

I've always kept a journal, usually writing it up at the beginning of each day. I do it for two reasons: one, to make a record I can refer to later (so the journals do do, partly, what a diary does), and two, because writing whatever comes to mind limbers me up and gets me into the writing zone. Over the years, I've published perhaps a dozen or so pieces extracted from my journals, but I never planned to do much more than that – or at least that was what I thought until I stumbled across Christa Wolf's *One Day a Year: 1960–2000* and *One Day a Year:*

2001–2011. Wolf's books, consisting of her diary for 27 September each year, got me thinking. Why couldn't I take one day from each year of my journals, starting with the year I'd arrived in Northern Ireland? That way I would make a book – though mine would be smaller and more parochial than Wolf's, and the days would not be the same day each year; they would need to be different – which would tell the story of the place where I'd found myself accidentally living as it morphed from the Troubles to the Good Friday Agreement to Brexit, decades later. Out of these slivers, a picture of Northern Ireland would arise, as experienced by a Panglossian who was so certain that the tide was flowing in the right (progressive) direction, he failed to see that it was actually flowing in the wrong direction.

Of course, this was never a story I'd planned to witness, let alone write about.

When I got the commission for what became *The Glass Curtain*, I was living in London, where I'd mostly lived since 1958 when my parents relocated there from Dublin. I knew I didn't want to make a series of research trips to Ireland and then write the book in London. I wanted to be embedded in the place for the whole process, the researching and the writing, and so we moved, temporarily we thought, my wife and I and our two young children, to County Fermanagh in 1989, imagining we'd stay a few months, or at most a year. However, everything took longer than expected and we had to extend our stay. The book took two years, and by the time it was done we had a home and our children were settled, and so we decided we'd stay until our children had finished school and various good things that were happening had run their course. And this was our understanding until the Christmas before the millennium – by this stage we had five children and we'd been in Northern Ireland eleven years – when my wife spotted that our local church was selling husband-and-wife double burial plots for buttons. We should snaffle one, she said. We should just accept we were never returning to London and we were going to die where we were. She was right.

Alan Bennett, describing how he prepares his diaries for publication, writes: 'I've not had any scruples about improving and editing, though I've never altered the tone or the sentiments of what I've written at the time.'[1] I've followed his injunction (or so I'd like to believe). I have, however, where I thought I needed more, occasionally added new material; this content is always italicised, while the journal entries are not.

The children of writers have a special burden. I have chosen not to name mine but to identify them by their place in the family. In some places, in order to anonymise, I have changed people's names or other details.

1 'Diaries 1980–1990', *Writing Home*, Alan Bennett, London, 1994, p. 97.

The Fall of Communism, the End of History (Not) (Friday, 10 November 1989)

I drove to Belfast with the radio on, BBC Radio 4. The morning news was almost entirely about the Iron Curtain and its often predicted, yet still somehow, now it's happening, unbelievable collapse.

Yesterday, Thursday, the East Berlin party chief, Günter Schabowski, held a press conference and said that, starting at midnight, East Germans would be free to leave the country at any point along the border, including the crossing points through the wall in Berlin. This morning, as I learnt from listening to *Today* with Peter Hobday and Sue MacGregor while driving through the murk (some rain, some wind, an Irish autumn day, predictable and hackneyed, the kind that required only intermittent use of the wipers), East German bulldozers had opened and were opening new crossing points to allow East Berliners to go west. A comment on the events unfolding in Germany was sought, of course, from our beloved prime minister, Mrs Thatcher, and in her perplexing, caressing and, according to many, seductive voice (entirely the creation of a speech coach: her real register, like her nature, is spiky and shrill), the PM spoke of what was happening in Germany as 'a great day for freedom'. A great day for freedom! Well, yeah, technically it's true – East Germans are free to go west – but linguistically the comment was pure dreck, utterly banal. Why can't politicians go for newly minted language? But no, they won't.

Sometime after nine (*Desert Island Discs* on the radio; Sue Lawley's guest was Ian Botham: stodgy, charmless, crass – a philistine mediocrity) I got to West Belfast (damp streets, grey sky, to my left the mountains in the distance, dark and brooding) and things were flowing nicely. And then they were not flowing nicely any more, and I had to stop. In front of me, a mechanical diplodocus straddled the road, and from its long neck there dangled a heavy metal sheath (actually bombproof cladding) that was going to be first lifted, then flown, and finally dropped onto the internal brick structure of a section of the 'peace line' that ran beside the road, one of dozens of similar barriers that have been constructed since the start of the Troubles to keep antagonistic communities apart in Northern Ireland.

I turned off the engine and looked at the dashboard clock. I was on my way to meet a psychiatrist to discuss the psychological effects of the Troubles. I'd always assumed the violence must raise the levels of anxiety and depression. But I was wrong. Psychological well-being in Northern Ireland (measured in terms of suicides, para suicides, prescriptions for sleeping tablets and so on) was about the same as anywhere else in the United Kingdom, and the psychiatrist who was going to enlighten me further about this counter-intuitive fact was, at that moment, as I sat waiting for the peace line to be reinforced, sitting in his room in the hospital, having agreed, despite his incredibly busy schedule, to talk to me. Only now it looked as if I was going to be late, in which case I'd probably miss my slot and miss having what I was sure was going to be a fascinating conversation that would hugely enhance the book I had come to Northern Ireland to write; and if I wanted another shot, I'd have to arrange a new time, which would mean a second 180-mile journey from Enniskillen to West Belfast and back again. What a drag. Why couldn't it have been a different day, a different hour, when this bit of the peace line was slated for augmentation? I was a writer writing a book with a delivery date, for Christ's sake, and I shouldn't be held up like this in the street as I made my way to my very important appointment.

In another part of the brain, a separate compartment from the place where I fret about my timetable – this is a place of perennial anxiety: I hate to be late – a completely different set of thoughts was in play. In Germany over the last few months, crowds regularly gathered on both sides of the Berlin Wall to shout 'Democracy, now or never!' and 'Free passage for free citizens!' but in Belfast and elsewhere in Northern Ireland, as far as I was aware, the peace lines had been wanted and welcomed, and no crowds had ever gathered and asked for them to be torn down. And as I'd heard earlier on the radio, at that very moment, while I was watching one kind of wall being improved and strengthened in Belfast, the wall in Berlin was being bulldozed. Here was an opportunity for a compare-and-contrast riff – *Germany and Europe: forwards; Northern Ireland and the United Kingdom: backwards* – and therefore, I thought, I should observe, record to memory what was happening, and later I could use this material in the book I was writing. I could see this made sense, and so I tried. I looked around. What did I see?

A man sauntered past. He carried a couple of SPAR plastic bags. Through the thin plastic I thought I could make out bread, milk, sausages and tins of something, perhaps rice pudding. A dog, a heavy old Labrador, waddled by. I noticed a couple of old ladies with wheeled shopping baskets, both in coats and hats and scarves and gloves (they were so well insulated they were almost like walking duvets).

Finally, I noticed the downstairs window of a terraced house across the road from the peace line, the lace curtain opening a crack and an old female face peering out at the unfolding scene, in just the same way, I imagined, as she might have looked at a neighbour who was drunk and staggering, or a couple who should definitely not be courting walking arm in arm. Behind and ahead, a sense of traffic piling up; the tinny sound of music on the radios of some of the waiting cars mingled with the heavier mechanical sounds of the crane, its diesel engine churning, its taut cabling running over wheels and pinging, the lifting system harrumphing like breath and the sheath clattering, swinging and banging as it was dropped carefully and very slowly over the brick support and lowered towards the ground. It was like being in the theatre and seeing a flat being flown in during a scene change. And then the change was done. The chains were detached. With further harrumphing, the diplodocus crawled away. I turned on my engine. Botham came back. The traffic started to move. I was on my way.

I was late for my appointment but the psychiatrist, when I explained, was blithe and understanding. It was Belfast, West Belfast, and one was always being held up, he said – by checkpoints, or bombs, or because they were working on the peace line. That's how it went. He didn't mind my being late in the slightest and he had time to spare. I sat in his small office and we talked, and when we were done he gathered some academic papers by psychiatrists for me to take away and read.

I left and retraced my route. I passed the peace line I'd seen earlier with its new cladding. No sign of the diplodocus. I drove home, and when I walked into the kitchen in our flat I found my oldest daughter back from school (she was at the table in her school uniform: her uniform is blue and worn with a sash; she has started at the Integrated School in Enniskillen) along with my wife and two sons. I was asked what sort of day I had had. Interesting, I said. I'd had to stop, I said, and watch a crane drop a huge piece of metal casing onto a section of a peace line in West Belfast, while hundreds of miles to the east a border was being demolished, a moment of synchronicity out of which I might be able to wring some interesting copy.

What was Checkpoint Charlie, asked my oldest daughter. She'd overheard the words on the news and didn't know what they meant. As onions for the tomato sauce were chopped and gently fried, and as the water for the pasta was heated on the stove, I did my best to explain. In Berlin in the 1960s, I said, a wall had been built down the middle of the city and Checkpoint Charlie was one of the crossing points in that wall where people could go from one side to the other, from east to west and vice versa; at the same time, it was also a symbol of the Cold War. My knowledge, I realised as I burbled on, was vacuous and shallow, being mostly derived from photographs I'd seen in newspapers and on television of the Berlin Wall and the fearsome German Democratic Republic guards who guarded it, articles I'd read about hairy escapes via tunnels under the wall and spy films about the Cold War, particularly the film of John le Carré's novel *The Spy Who Came in from the Cold*, which I'd loved (with Richard Burton as Alec Leamas: weary, cynical, noble, incredible). My ignorance was staggering, but mercifully went unnoticed.

★

A few days after my Belfast trip and my meeting with the diplodocus, I met a local journalist in Enniskillen who told me how he'd recently gone to watch a small road between Fermanagh and Cavan being blocked with dragon's teeth to stop the IRA using it, although everyone else would also be stopped from using it. There were Garda Síochána and Royal Ulster Constabulary (RUC) policemen present; they all knew one another and they all chatted happily as the army engineers got the blocks in place. The policemen's conversations were about how in Germany the wall had fallen, but in Ireland it was the same old, same old. Some of us in Ireland, the police postulated, might want a new future, but most of us preferred to say 'To hell with the future, let's get on with the past …'

and so we just went on doing what we had always done; we went on erecting barriers to maintain our separation.

As we said goodbye, my journalist friend gave me a postcard a guard had given him at the road-blocking he'd attended. The postcard showed a border road blocked with concrete dragon's teeth, across which was printed 'Welcome to Fermanagh'. As the policeman handed the card to my friend he'd said that roads shouldn't be closed.

'And you know what I thought when he said that?' said my journalist friend. 'If the police are the only ones making sense, it's a sure sign that your politics really are totally fucked.'

PRIME
RETAIL UNIT
FOR SALE

How to Buy a House in an Afternoon (Sunday, 28 October 1990)

The notion *The Glass Curtain* could be written in a year was wrong; the book is taking longer, of course. Everything always does. On top of that, things are happening. I might be making some films for the BBC. In light of everything, my wife suggested we should give up the flat where we're living (the old nursery at the top of Rossfad, a big house overlooking Lough Erne) and buy a modest house and then, when we leave and return to London, we can sell it.

Decision made, my wife went house-hunting. This involved walking the length of the high street in Enniskillen from one bridge to the other and looking in the windows of the half-dozen or so estate agents, seeing what inexpensive properties were for sale and getting their particulars. She found three, and all that then remained to be done was to whittle three down to one, and yesterday, Sunday, we did exactly that.

It was a classic Fermanagh day: damp, wet, with a grey sky which had been lowered to just a few yards above our heads. Richard Pierce, the architect, who has agreed to help us, appeared in his car, and we put the children in our car, and together we drove in convoy, the plan being that we would look at all three and pick one.

First up was a cottage on a lane out at Monea – a knobbly house built for small, indomitable, hard-working rural labourers, with buckled rooms and tiny windows. The garden, rather than being at the back, side or front of the cottage, was on the other side of the public road that runs in front of the cottage. Our children, said Richard, would be going backwards and forwards, from house to garden and garden to house, across the road all the time and that ruled the house out. We agreed.

The second building was in Letterbreen – a lovely old house built for a minister and his family, airy rooms with pine floors and fireplaces and great casement windows, which looked into the lovely garden where bitter-smelling Irish yews grew. There was a return at the back, but between it and the front part there was a gap that ran from the roof all the way to the foundations. The two parts of the house had drifted so far apart, said Richard, he doubted they could be reunited. It was more likely than not that the whole house would have to come down and an entirely new one be built. This we could not afford. We left.

Third and last was Derryhillagh County Primary School, nestled in the hills above Enniskillen. The grounds: about an acre; sycamore trees; a grassy, overgrown playground; a bicycle shed with a buckled green corrugated roof; a dry toilet with wooden toilet seats and a void below to hold the waste, with furnace doors at the back that opened to get the night soil out. The school building, outside: white pebble-dashed walls, a Dutch bow-backed roof, Jacobean chimneys and huge metal-framed windows; separate entrances for boys and girls. The school building, inside: two huge high-ceilinged classrooms with blackboards, dado rails and Irish pine floors; behind and beside the classrooms, a corridor, with a polished concrete floor and swing doors that still swung 180 degrees on their ingeniously designed hinges, and cloakrooms with the original coat hooks. It was a building properly designed, with every detail intended to advance its function and then constructed to last. That was palpable in the structure.

It was also a mess. The last class had left in 1973, since when it had functioned as a furniture store, a photographic studio, a darkroom (old bottles of fixer in the sink giving off an acrid reek and rolls of photographic paper that, now damp, had lost their lustre), a sheep house and a workshop. Old bits of agricultural machinery (bailers, grass-cutters, shearing units) as well as engine parts were everywhere, plus tools, a workbench and drums of Castrol. Sheep and bat droppings were ground into the pine floor. The glass in most of the windows was gone, with birds flying in and out.

To us it appeared derelict, unsalvageable. Richard demurred. What we could see were merely cosmetic problems and easy to rectify, he said. What mattered was whether the building was sound. Richard thought, with the windows all being broken, the building had stayed aired; and a building which had stayed aired was much more likely to have remained dry and therefore sound. Richard then went to each corner of each classroom where he tested the quality of the pine floor (and his thesis) by jumping up and down. The floors performed beautifully. They held up. This proved it. More than likely, no damp, no rot. And given the state of the floors, he continued, it followed that the whole building, in his opinion, was probably sound. It was a lovely structure, he added, well built to high standards, and with very little work (and he explained what was involved) it could easily and cheaply be made habitable. Obviously, a survey was required (the mortgage lender would demand one, and if the building didn't pass muster we wouldn't be able to buy anyway) but in his opinion this was the house to buy. My wife said she'd ring the estate agent first thing Monday morning. Someone in the office, she said, had already indicated there were no other interested parties. If we offered the asking price, £18,000, the old schoolhouse was ours, she understood. So, we have.

The Journey Home (Monday, 7 January 1991)

We'd been in London for Christmas and New Year. We no longer live there – we live in Ireland now, or Northern Ireland to be precise – and when the holiday finished we left London and drove north, heading for home. The M1 was damp and dismal and wretched. The tarmac and the chevrons and the signage all seemed saturated with sullen post-festivity let-down, and they all appeared to signal that there was nothing ahead but the grind of work through January.

Somewhere in the middle of middle England we stopped at a service station. The cafeteria was monstrous in size, and terrible Christmas music was burbling out of the Tannoy system. Its huge glass windows, which overlooked the motorway, were covered with condensation; thus, we were deprived of the magnificent view. Yes, whoever designed this service station believed that traffic thundering past was what every diner would want to gaze out on as they refreshed themselves. It must have made sense to someone once, but it made no sense to me now.

We had sandwiches and terrible coffee and regretted what we had spent on what was so poor. Then we went for fuel. The petrol forecourt was full of big gruff men in woollen hats refuelling white vans and shouting to one another about the terrible state of the British motorway system. They all seemed unhappy, resentful and chippy, but then why wouldn't they be? Every day they're out driving on a road network that's not fit for purpose, and any contact with it is a downer. Their mood was contagious. Spirits suitably lowered, we resumed our journey.

South of Liverpool we turned left and drove across the top of Wales (these roads were particularly empty, and there was an even stronger sense of post-Christmas anomie than on the motorway in England); then it was across the Menai Strait on the marvellous suspension bridge, the turbid waters below us a gunmetal grey in the failing wintry late-afternoon light (it was about three o'clock), and onto Anglesey Island. Now, driving on, driving west, we found ourselves in a different world, a world of farm walls, farm fields, farm cottages, farm animals – all in all, a strong sense of the rural. Eventually we reached our destination, Holyhead, with its unsettling dual feel: prosperous and affluent on the one hand, decaying and failing on the other. The flourishing bit had buildings where the windows had gold writing on the insides and the doors had proper brass knockers and ornate letter boxes. Inside these buildings worked members of the professional classes – accountants, solicitors, chartered surveyors. There were also a couple of good-looking banks. The other bit, the depressed, decrepit bit, was full of boarded-up buildings, dismal shops and rubbish-filled gutters. On balance, there was more in Holyhead that was declining than was thriving.

We drove on to the harbour (hawsers, bollards, seagulls, empty sheds, rusting plant, desolate quays) and found our ferry (huge, hulking, with an enormous superstructure – so enormous I couldn't understand why it hadn't toppled over). It had an Irish name and would take us to Dún Laoghaire.

Once on board and out of the car and onto the passenger decks, there was a smell of old seawater, old Guinness, old stewed tea and, in odd corners and in all the toilets, the reek of new vomit, sour, throat-catching. We found seats (plastic, sticky and smelling of sweat) and settled down. The ferry pulled out, clanking and groaning malevolently in its bowels, the cacophony reminding me of ghost rides at funfairs, with their inexplicable, malevolent, dread-inducing mechanical noises. Outside the windows, Holyhead's quayside slipped past, stone-built and obdurate, and then the Irish Sea slid into view, grey and equally obdurate. We all had fish and chips (old batter, flaky, dry fish, surprisingly good chips) and then promenaded around the decks. It was dark now, no lights either behind or ahead, just utter, unrelenting darkness everywhere; there was a piercing wind, which blew from the east and the north, and it was obvious it was going to freeze.

We made landfall at Dún Laoghaire. The street lights were glowing weakly; evening was well on. The streets were dry and empty and chilled by the same icy wind we'd felt out at sea. Few people about, and those who were, were well swaddled. We drove north through the prosperous southside quarters – houses lit up like aquariums in which swam householders, soft furnishings, Christmas trees. The city centre – brightly lit windows, slightly garish displays, sullen huddles of Dubliners at the bus stops. A sense of commercial retreat and declining expectations, seediness and evaporating gentility. This was not the capital of a place of prosperity. The northside next, with its endless red-brick houses, dark, sepulchral, tragic. Then we crossed the magic line separating city and non-city, not knowing we had crossed it until after we were over it, and found ourselves with silent fields stretching away to our left and right; and we were cruising through the dark in our small metal box, our headlamps burrowing ahead, lighting up wraiths of freezing air and dustings of frost on the tarmac below. The temperature was dropping. I kept the blower on, full blast. Its heat made everyone drowsy. Talk stopped. Gradually I sensed the family's breathing synchronising as they dropped off. By Kells I was the only one awake.

The way into Cavan town was down a hill, steep and curving. Absolutely no one around. The cold and the hour had driven everyone home. I went slowly as I descended, my right foot covering the brake, and I noticed, displacing the calm that had existed until now, an internal thickening. This was an old feeling, a familiar feeling; it always came on the home journey at this point – the hill in Cavan town its marker – because, the hill once reached, the knowledge followed that the border between south and north was looming. It was a sort of loose pre-emptive anxiety that had no basis in past personal experience but was nonetheless a thing. The border was a contested space: things happened there; none had happened to us, to me, but the body, if not the mind, knew things could go wrong there and was preparing for that possibility by putting me on my mettle.

After Cavan we forked right at Butlers Bridge, onto the Clones Road – a straight run between higher hedgerows, where the dark seemed even darker. Doubtless that was an illusion. We passed the entrance to an old estate with its gates closed and small houses with no lights on. The road was empty. I had seen nothing for miles now. No traffic. No pedestrians. But you never knew who or what you might meet. And there was frost. I dropped my speed and crawled along, peering where my headlights probed, eyes straining.

And then … actually, come to think of it – where were we? The border was so convoluted here that one passed between jurisdictions without knowing, every fifty yards it seemed. At that moment I didn't actually know if I was in the south or the north. And then I did know because, ahead of me, appeared the Leggykelly Inn – a modern construction, shoddily built, ugly, unwelcoming, set at the back of a nasty pitted apron of hardcore. It was in the south, wasn't it, the Leggykelly Inn …? And as my mind floundered and tried to remember and failed, that was when I saw on the road, right where the hardcore stopped … Oh God … a red light and a sign propped up. I couldn't read the words on the triangle but I could guess: 'Stop Checkpoint'. I slowed. Stopped. In the gloom, along the verge, on the hardcore, figures milling. According to the rumour mill, the IRA had been known to set their own checkpoints along this road, sometimes in front of this pub. Could this … might this be …?

As I lowered the window I tried to decipher who was approaching. It was a uniform for sure. But not an army uniform. This was not a soldier. Ah. This was a policeman. 'Do you have any identification?' The accent was Cork to my ears. Oh, right. Not RUC. It was a guard. Well, that was all right. I'd never been asked to get out and open my boot by a guard. Or quizzed about my address. Guards were different, easier. There was less friction with them. Actually, no friction. They even exuded pity that one lived in benighted Ulster.

The face loomed closer. A broad face. Creased. A big nose. Early fifties. Male. Probably a sergeant. I fished out my wallet and then my licence from my wallet and passed it through the window. A torch came on. The sergeant – if he was a sergeant – played the beam on the licence and then my face. Genial questions followed. Where had I been, where was I going, et cetera.

'I've been in England with my family,' I said. 'We took the ferry from Holyhead earlier, and now we're driving home. We live near Enniskillen.' I gave my home address, which was unnecessary as it was on the licence. But that's what you do when it's the middle of the night and a uniform is asking questions, even if it's a genial uniform.

The beam of the torch lifted and lightly skimmed the faces in the back. 'It's a long drive,' he said.

The torch went off.

'Not long till we're home,' I said.

He handed back the licence. I put it in my wallet and the wallet back in my pocket. Many of my friends favoured the back slit in the sun visor as the licence holder – with checkpoints so frequent, it meant the licence would always be there in the car when needed – but I preferred to keep mine close. I was frightened of licence theft.

'Is the checkpoint beyond Wattle Bridge open?' I asked. This was the British army checkpoint a couple of miles beyond the border, which we had to get through to get home; it was set back so it couldn't be fired on from the south. From time to time it had been closed, hence my question – and if anyone would know it was this policeman, for surely the guards and the soldiers must know about each other's activities. The British army soldiers in their checkpoint must know about this Garda Síochána checkpoint outside the Leggykelly.

'Oh, yes,' he replied authoritatively.

'Goodnight,' I said.

'Goodnight.'

I wound up the window. As I eased away I saw the shining eyes of armed men. The road beyond dark, convoluted. Underneath the car, the tarmac of the N54 rumbled.

At some point I passed from the south to the north. I'd heard it said the tarmac in the north made a different sound and had a different feel than that in the south (tarmac cognoscenti could 'hear' this, just as soft-drink aficionados could distinguish between Coca-Cola and Pepsi at a blind tasting – or so it was alleged), but I felt nothing, heard nothing. I just moved, everything sounding uniform, until there it was, the bulky outline of the checkpoint at Wattle Bridge, an iron and steel fortress bristling with aerials and garlanded with wire. I slowed and crawled closer … Something not right … It was too still, too silent, too dark. Closer again … Normally the barrier would be down and the high steel gates behind would be pinned back and one could see in, see the checkpoint's innards, see the airlock, see the block houses with the gun slits, see the barracks where the soldiers lived, see the road running through the middle that one had to drive along in order to get through to the other side (with checkpoints, one really does pass *through* them not *by* them); but tonight, the barrier was down and the high steel gates behind were not pinned back. Tonight, instead, the gates behind the barrier were closed over. Oh no, the checkpoint was shut.

I stopped at the stop line and looked at the high steel wall the gates made. It was the middle of the night, I thought, or actually very early in the morning. There wasn't a lot of traffic around, or any traffic, actually. Presumably, I thought, that's why the checkpoint was closed. But it was manned. There were soldiers inside. There had to be. And, what's more, I could see a sign illuminated by a spotlight on a pole. If I wanted assistance, said the sign, I was to speak into the intercom. Fair enough. I'd disembark. Approach the intercom. Press the bell. Intercoms always had bells, didn't they? A soldier would answer. I'd explain I needed to get through, needed to get home. He'd understand. Of course he would. That's how this would play out. I couldn't see how it could go any other way.

I got out and quietly closed the car door. I inclined my head, listened. Could I hear anything inside the fortress? Nothing. I moved carefully over the frost-dusted road to the gate and the intercom, a box with a grubby ridged cover over the speaker and buttons. *Do I dare?* Into my mind came a sliver of information I didn't know I'd stored away. A little over a year earlier, just before Christmas 1989 the IRA had attacked the British army checkpoint near Rosslea – a few miles east from where I was standing – with machine guns, grenades, anti-tank rockets and a flamethrower, killing two and wounding two. The knowledge that this had happened very recently, and at this time of year, was the sort of knowledge that would make anyone inside a checkpoint nervous, and when someone turned up in the middle of the night, as I had, they'd be doubly nervous, wouldn't they?

Another sliver that came floating in was of very recent provenance – it was an article in a newspaper I'd read on the ferry only a few hours earlier. On 30 December 1990, just a few days earlier, Fergal Caraher – a member of the Provisional IRA and Sinn Féin – was killed by two Royal Marines very close to the Cullyhanna checkpoint in South Armagh. According to the report I'd read (a thoroughly infuriating piece full of obscurities and lacunae), Caraher was in a car with his brother, Michael, when the soldiers from the checkpoint, believing a marine was being carried away by the Caraher brothers on the bonnet of their car (an allegation witnesses vehemently disputed), opened fire and killed Fergal. Those were all the details I had, but they were enough. Checkpoints, the article confirmed, were where accidents happened, and who wanted to be involved in an accident? Not I.

Of course, I wasn't Caraher, and I didn't have his profile, but I couldn't help wondering – what would the soldiers think when the bell woke them, and then they heard me asking for the gates to be opened? Probably nothing. On the whole, whatever you did in Northern Ireland, you were mostly fine. Mostly. Now and again things went awry – how could they not when young men with guns were involved? – and for most of the time, after things had gone wrong, you either forgot or ignored them. However, every now and again there came a moment when something buried – i.e., not forgotten but repressed – suddenly came whooshing up to the mind's surface, after which corrective action inevitably followed. You were about to do A but then you thought, no, bad idea, I'll do B – with, in this case, A being me pressing the buzzer and B being me getting back into the car and driving to a checkpoint that was actually open, if I could find one. That's the genius of violence: it produces real behavioural change. Stories of violence crawl into the psyche, and then, once they're in there, they do their fiendish work. As happened now.

I got back in the car, turned, drove down to the N54 and headed for Clones, the next checkpoint going east. Darkness and nothing, just the rumble of the engine and the turning of the fan in the heater and high dark hedgerows to the left and right unfurling like bolts of cloth. After a bit I saw a red light and the dark shapes of armed men milling. Oh, for Christ's sake. Again? I stopped, put down the window, heard an Ulster voice. A soldier approached in fatigues, his face streaked with blacking, his eyes shining very white in the middle. What had happened with the guards was repeated: the licence came out, the torch went on, et cetera, et cetera. The only difference was the tone. This guy was belligerent and had none of the charm of the Corkonian who had preceded him.

After the licence had been examined and the facts confirmed (London, ferry, Dún Laoghaire), I explained that the Wattle Bridge checkpoint was closed and asked if we'd get through at the Clones checkpoint.

'You'll get through at Clones,' he assured me.

'Are you sure?' I pressed. (In my mind, I was wondering if we'd have to wait till after dawn before anything opened.)

'Into Clones and turn left,' he said.

Well, that was all fine and dandy, except for the fact that when we got into Clones (rundown, threatening, a bit sinister), *there wasn't one sign for the Kilturk checkpoint*. Not one. Some joker had removed them all. A strike against the Brits and their war machine, which probably seemed funny when it was done but wasn't nearly so funny at 3 a.m. in the morning. Eventually I saw a woman, the first civilian I'd spotted for a good while, who in turn saw me and – not liking what she saw – turned up an alley. If I lost her, we would never find our way home. I wound down the window of the car and bellowed after her, 'Kilturk?' and then watched as she stopped, spun about, returned. We weren't trouble, just lost. I could see it on her face; she understood what we were and what we were was no threat.

'Kilturk,' she said, 'straight on.'

She was right. It was just down the road. The gates too were pulled over. And this checkpoint too was closed. Oh, Christ. No, this had to stop. I would get out. I would use the intercom. The soldiers would open the fucking gates. They would let us through.

I got out and walked over to the gates. Ah. I hadn't thought of this. No intercom, nor any information about what those needing assistance should do. The only sign was this one:

We apologise for the delay
Please do not blame us
Blame the Terrorists

with this, which was slightly smaller, alongside it:

Please take your litter home with you

Oh, for fuck's sake. Where was I supposed to go now? Obviously, the next checkpoint, but wasn't that the one at Rosslea, the one the IRA had very recently attacked? With a flamethrower? What were the chances that one would be closed too? High. And what was the next checkpoint going east? Was it at Aughnacloy? That was another one to avoid. All sorts of dire things had happened there. Perhaps I should head in the other direction, towards Derry? As my thoughts churned and I tried to work out where to go and what to do, I heard – what? The creak of a boot? I went still while my heart raced. People were moving on the other side of the gate. I heard metal grinding (it sounded like a deadbolt being pulled open), and then one of the steel gates opened a fraction and a gun barrel came out and introduced itself to me.

'Dip your fucking lights,' a voice shouted. I could see through the gap a soldier with a rifle and, behind him, another soldier, and he was doing the talking. He must be the corporal, I decided. He was the man I had to get past.

I went back to the car and dipped the headlamps.

What now? The corporal squinted through the crack between the gates and began to call out my registration, his voice booming, truculent, sullen, and whomever he was calling to called the numbers and the letters of my car's registration back in a voice that was equally booming, truculent, sullen. Then the gates were churlishly closed over and locked again. I got back in the car and sat with the engine idling, the children sleeping, my wife now awake, watchful and perplexed, while my car's details were fed into a computer somewhere and cross-checked against the details already stored of the scores of border crossings I'd made since we moved to Northern Ireland.

After a while the gates were swung back. I looked forward and saw a lot of men crouched waiting inside, rifles to the shoulder, trained on the car.

'Okay.' It was my friend the corporal. I turned off my main beams and turned on my parking lights. I was about to put the car in gear when I noticed – right beside the checkpoint, in fact touching it – a house, and in the front window was a Christmas tree with lights draped along its branches.

We left the twinkling tree and entered the fortress, and as I crawled through all I saw were boot-polish-covered faces and the ends of the gun barrels, small Os glimmering palely.

'Where are we?' a child called sleepily from the back. 'Are we home yet?'

We emerged from the checkpoint's far side into a dark landscape, with a cold starry sky arching above us. 'Yes, nearly,' my wife whispered. 'It won't be long now.'

★

On the Monday after New Year in 1991 I had woken up in a country called England, a relatively well functioning, neo-liberal place where the rule of law prevailed and where, typically, the security services didn't either inhibit or control movement. After breakfast I popped my family into the car and we drove up the motorways. In Wales we took a ferry; in Dublin we disembarked. We drove out of Dublin and struck for the north where we'd just bought a house, though we weren't yet living in it; nothing impeded us until we reached Northern Ireland, a functioning democracy where the rule of law was observed, blah, blah, at which point I found I couldn't pass. I didn't mind. I was frustrated, of course, but I had internalised the narrative – republican violence and the use of Ireland (the south) by the terrorists as a place from which to launch attacks on the north had obliged the UK to adopt extraordinary measures in this part of the nation, to close most roads along the border between north and south and to only allow movement across that border at a limited number of checkpoints controlled by the British army. This was the narrative I had embedded within me, and even though I was frustrated and put out by what had happened, I wasn't aggrieved.

Now, however, decades having passed, and having had the experience of the open border between the north and the south of Ireland that came after the Good Friday Agreement, I don't think any more in terms of cause and effect – the IRA did X so the British government reacted by doing Y. Such thinking is too short-term, too technical and frankly stupid. I now think of the closed border rather as a symptom (and a morbid one at that) of the failure of statecraft, largely on the part of the UK and its politicians. They devised partition, though the Irish agreed and the unionists, on whose behalf partition was enacted in order to ensure a permanent Protestant majority in the north, applauded. Partition is never a good idea, but it's an even worse idea when it's mixed with sectarianism. It can only end in ugliness, as it did, an ugliness we euphemistically call the Troubles.

A proper democratic country should be open but this one wasn't – at least not on the night I was trying to get home with my family. A proper democratic country ought not to be one where one could only go in or come out through British-army-controlled checkpoints and where all the other roads were closed. It made sense back in 1991 but now, hindsight being the fine thing it is, I see that night in County Cavan as a sign of failure, state failure, the blame for which can largely be laid at the feet of the country that ought to have known better.

40
42

In Belfast: a Hot Night and the Morning After (August 1992)

The day was a baking one, and the whole city was stunned by the pitiless sunlight and the unrelenting heat, and come night, the city's inhabitants, of whom I was temporarily one, fell onto their beds, relieved, exhausted, yearning for oblivion.

In the week when I'm in Belfast working (returning to Fermanagh at the weekends), I lodge in an old house in a street of old houses – could they be Regency? – which by the standards of the times are a rarity. Much of the older parts of the city have been levelled by the forces of national liberation and the developers, who appear to me to be working hand in hand to remake this lovely Victorian urban jewel that is Belfast into an Irish version of Swindon. My bedroom is at the top, tucked under the roof. In the day, the thick old slates had heated like Victorian irons set in the embers of a fire, and come night, they gave back their stored-up heat to the room just below, where I lay on my low bed on top of the covers. I had the window open but there was no breeze coming in. The air was turgid, oppressive, enervating. I kept surfacing into half-wakefulness and sinking back again. My dreams were febrile, full of clamours and loud alarms and dangers of an unspecified but deeply menacing nature.

Toward 3 a.m., when the night was darkest and stillest and sleep supposedly deepest and densest, I became aware – was this a dream? No, it was the actual sounds – of something smashing, boots thumping on the stairs, my bedroom door violently opening, the light switch flicking and a voice screaming, very loud, very close …

I was confused and only partly awake, still swimming up towards the surface, but the subconscious part of my brain offered this intelligence: the speaker, who was male, was from the English Midlands, Coventry or Stoke, Wolverhampton or Birmingham, somewhere like that, and he was working class. Having established his social category (and that I did this first and automatically speaks volumes about my indwelling class consciousness), I properly tuned in to my visitor's voice. I realised he was terrified, and having recognised his terror, something in me curdled (you could call this the contagion response) and I became as sick with terror, nausea and fear as I sensed he was.

I surfaced fully and opened my eyes. I saw a British soldier, in fatigues, blacking on his face, an enormous gun in his hands. Guns always tend to be much bigger than I expect when I see them close up, which is an experience I often have in Belfast, where I regularly see soldiers with guns – on average, eight, ten, even twelve times a day. The soldier was continuing to shout at me. I began to process his words. The news wasn't good. Actually, it was bad. No, it was terrible. There was a van at the end of the street, and inside the van there was a bomb, and it was a very big bomb, a humungous bomb, actually, and if it went off … curtains! The soldier said that several times. If the bomb inside the van went off – 'Curtains! Curtains! Curtains!' No street, no house, no him, no me … Just like that, we'd all be gone.

Next, in my head, in my body (where do these sensations lodge?): serene silence and stillness, and a heady and intoxicating mix of the opposite of panic. Not non-panic but actual anti-panic, which, as I'd just discovered, was a thing. I'd heard others speak of this – the calm that subdues one in a crisis and muffles terror – but had never quite believed it was true and had never myself known this sensation either, but now, as if by magic, it had come. Just like that. A miracle.

'Anyone else in the house?' the soldier shouted.

My voice stole out quietly as I replied. The anti-panic was working. My landlord was in London, I explained, but his partner, E., was in the front bedroom, next door to my room, with her son, a toddler.

'Get her … wake her … must get her out!' shouted the soldier.

My inner pilot issued his instructions; they ran down my nervous system as impulses and my muscles responded with alacrity. I got up and went out onto the landing and banged into E.'s bedroom. The room was hot and stuffy like mine. E. and her baby were in bed, asleep, mother and child merged to make one unit, their breath soughing in and out. The curtains were open, and light from the street lights outside poured in, and by their sickly yellow glow I noticed E. was wearing a black lacy choker, perhaps for her infant son to hold on to. Through the window, coming up from the street outside, I could also hear our neighbours streaming from their houses and the sound of gruff male soldierly voices barking orders in the same frantic tone as the soldier behind me had adopted when he was in my bedroom. The noise from below was troubling, roiling, muted yet thunderous, so loud and so quiet at the same time somehow, and as my body processed what it was hearing – the sound of communal fear – the anti-panic vanished and my stomach re-curdled. Terror, it seemed, was not a static thing but an ever-evolving, ever-escalating thing that started terrible and then, incredibly, got worse. Then the anti-panic coursed back in and filled me up again.

'Get up!' I said, shaking E. 'We must get out.'

'Now!' screamed the squaddie, who had followed me in. E. sat up, pale and white except for the choker, her infant in her arms, hair on her shoulders.

'Out!' shouted the soldier. 'Now!'

We flew down the stairs together and rushed past the splintered front door (the soldier had used his giant rifle, I realised as I passed, to break it down) and into the street. Here was a scene. Every front door of every house was open, many broken, splinters and door debris everywhere. And out through the gaping doors and into the street, my neighbours, in their night clothes, cascaded, a torrent of appalled, frightened, confused humanity, urged on by soldiers frenziedly gesticulating, now waving in the direction they wanted everyone to hurry, now waving the other way at our collective nemesis, the abandoned van sunk on its axles (the papers the following day said the explosive load was three-and-a-half-thousand pounds of fertiliser and fuel), its hazard lights winking evilly. From behind the van and out of sight, came the River Lagan's reek, estuarine and muddy.

We surged away, huddled, anxious – E. with her infant son cradled in her arms, myself and all the other evacuees – in the direction the soldiers had pointed. I had no shoes, and the paving stones under my soles were warm and gritty. I was tired and blank and befuddled until we reached the Ulster Hall, when I found myself thinking, *Oh, it's the Ulster Hall. They've sent us to the Ulster Hall.* It was a place I knew something about. Edward Carson had spoken here against Rome Rule and for Ulster staying British. Ian Paisley had spoken here too, also against Rome Rule and for Ulster staying British. All the great unionists and loyalists had fulminated here. But Stiff Little Fingers, the great Ulster punk band, had also played here, demanding a better Ulster for everyone, an alternative Ulster. Like everything in Northern Ireland, the Ulster Hall is a mixed story, a place that contains within itself all our local contradictions. Obdurate politicians and visionary musicians who wanted to remake their homeland had both found temporary shelter in the old beast of a building.

We went inside. Civil-defence types (tweedy, serious, conservative, all straight out of a Philip Larkin poem, only with Ulster accents) gave us tea and sandwiches – cheese and scallion on white bread, quite nice, though the white bread did tend to stick to the roof of the mouth and had to be scraped away with a fingernail – and clothes and shoes. E. rang her mother, who rang her brother, who, as it happened, was staying nearby in a flat he was decorating. He appeared in his car and fetched us back there. The flat was in an old Belfast merchant's mansion: high ceilings, stucco decorations laid on thick, like icing, black-painted pine floors, marble fireplaces, deep mantelpieces, speckled mirrors and an air of Victorian prosperity and the conviction that all would be well just as long as the right people were in charge – the right people being the kind of people who'd lived here in its heyday. A total redecoration was underway. The flat stank of paint and turpentine.

I was shown to a small room with a narrow single bed. I got between the clean, rough sheets. I still had my watch on. It was about 4.30 a.m. Since I'd been woken, ninety minutes had passed, and in such a short time so much had happened. Through the single sash window I spotted glimmering in the east. Dawn was coming. In the distance, then, *boom!* The window shuddered as if a terrible giant had huffed hard at it, and I had the distinct sense of the giant's hands inside my entrails, tossing my organs lightly, like salad leaves. The controlled explosion, I realised. The bomb was neutralised, and now came the aftershock, the psychic equivalent of the Eustachian tubes clearing during the descent that follows an ascent – only it wasn't sound returning but a sort of retrospective understanding. It started with an image. With my mind's eye I saw the van sunk low on its axles, a bow-backed beast so heavily laden its belly grazed the ground, its hazard lights winking … and then, barrelling after the image, came the speculative thoughts. What if it had gone up before we'd escaped? Would the street have … would E. and I and her son have … would we have … survived? The curdling fear I'd felt previously was a liquid thing, but the moment I allowed myself to ponder *What if?* I got a new sensation, of weight and mass, heaviness and density. It was as if what had been fluid before had turned adamantine, like set concrete. I couldn't remember ever feeling something so hard within.

I lay and waited for sleep, but of course none arrived. The sky lightened further. A bird started to twitter in one of the green-leafed trees in the street, followed by a second and a third, and then the dawn chorus began in earnest. I heard a few distant revellers making their way drunkenly home – from an illicit shebeen, I presumed – and remembered with a throb of nostalgia the thrumming of the electric milk floats of my childhood dawns and the lovely *clink-clink* of milk bottles as the milkman filled the wire baskets that stood on the doorsteps of the houses in the tidy, torpid suburban street in Morden, in London, where I lived as a boy. There was a comforting sound, a sound that said all was well and would continue to be well. A lie, of course, and yet a pleasure at the same time to recollect.

In the later morning, when I got up, my eyes felt grimy and my head hurt from lack of sleep. E.'s brother drove us back to the house we'd fled in the night. We found our front door pulled shut but not locked – the lock was broken – and the windows mostly out, wooden splinters and puddles of glass on the pavements. Up and down the street, the sound of coarse bristles sweeping, and glass tinkling as it was dropped into metal dustbins, and voices shouting, and burly tradesmen doing their burly business as they repaired and restored and rectified. That was nice – the industry of the city's citizenry and her tradespeople who were so busily tidying up the mess. What was noticeable was the utter lack of rancour or disgruntlement about what had happened. No one was dwelling on the tiny matter of the mess having been made in the first place and who had made the mess and why they had made the mess and whether or not their making the mess was justified. Everyone just had to get on with it, ourselves included. E. and I spent the day sourcing a carpenter, a locksmith and a glazier. By dusk, the door and windows were fixed and the only physical sign of the bomb that remained were the glass particles that glittered for weeks afterwards between the paving stones in the street and in the gaps between the old Irish pine boards on every floor in the lovely old house where I lodged.

★

Some things that happened a long time ago have a mystery to them. They baffle. They puzzle. I see them with my inner eye. And then I scratch my head. Did it really happen? *That summer night in Belfast is one such event. I know it happened (notes were scribbled), yet it remains for me a dream – a bad dream, of course – and I have never been able to shake off that idea. Perhaps that's all part of the coping strategy. If it was all just a figment, there was never any danger.*

At the Violet Hour (Thursday, 7 October 1993)

Just before dusk, I carried my bicycle out the door of the building in Lower Crescent in Belfast where my new office is located and set it down on the pavement. Lower Crescent is a line of stucco-clad houses, late Georgian or early Victorian, with a little park in front. I heard voices, high and fluting, and I saw, around a bench in the park, half a dozen street drinkers were gathered, pot-bellied, thin-legged, passing a bottle one to the next, all excited, all talking over one another.

I smelt petrol fumes and tobacco, perfume and cooking oil, and the muddy edges of the lough on the edge of which Belfast sits. A group of girls passed with bare legs and brown made-up faces, all holding little silver bags, lively and excited, their heels clicking. A sense of imminence hung in the air, stirring and palpable. I decided that, instead of cycling, I'd walk to my new flat in Eglantine Avenue (I wasn't in the old Georgian house near the markets any more: I was in Belfast bedsit-land now), and as I walked I'd drink it in, the atmosphere of the violet hour.

I began to amble towards University Road. Ahead of me a group of youths in tracksuits and runners, Bacchanalian, boisterous, bumptious, were pulling lengths of wood from a skip and then mock sword-fighting. Cries of 'Take that!' and 'I'm hit' and 'I'm dying' mingled with the clatter of wood on wood. As I drew closer the swordsmen abruptly lost interest in their fighting; they turned and ran towards me, whacking every bit of street furniture they encountered with their swords (the noise of wood on metal was cacophonous) and whooping lustily with joy, their cries pure orgiastic release. They were so lost in this moment I don't think they saw me as they sped by.

At the end of Lower Crescent I turned left. More people streaming towards the city centre and their night on the tiles: I noticed loud voices, exaggerated gestures, gelled hair, short jackets, ironed jeans, well-shined shoes, and I had a sense that everyone was talking themselves into having a good evening. Queen's University rose on my left, Gothic and Gormenghastian but also surprisingly small.

In front of the university's gates was a pedestrian crossing. As I waited dutifully for the beeps I remembered being here in the summer, exactly here, on this very bit of pavement. It was graduation day – there were students and their proud families everywhere, and everyone was dressed up in gowns, mortar boards, suits, frocks, and all the women, it seemed, were in very difficult-to-walk-in shoes. And standing at this very spot was a middle-aged woman in a pink summer dress, her high heels lying discarded in the gutter, the soles of her stockinged feet grey with dust, so drunk she could barely stand up, and she was grasping the pole to which the pedestrian-crossing lights were fixed. She was weeping and her face was streaked with tears. I'd approached her and asked if I could help or do anything but she'd waved me away, shouting, 'It's too much, much too much.'

The beeps sounding, I crossed over. On the far side, the student union building, square, modern, hideous, with students in front milling about, some with cans and many already liquored up judging by their jostling, their exuberance, their bravado. There would be music in the union later, a band, a DJ, and a late bar too, and it was to these pleasures this crowd was hurrying.

I walked on, passing the bank with its ATM – or 'drink-link' in the vernacular of the young – in front of which snaked a line of young people who, one after the next, were withdrawing the money they'd spend over the evening ahead. On the other side of the road was the entrance to Botanic Gardens. Parties of young were streaming through with carry-outs, which they would drink inside, under the trees, while talking and smoking – the pulse of reggae from a carried boom box and the special atmosphere when the young are out and pleasure-bent drifted across to me. Belfast might be known as a death town, but it is also a party town.

Three girls in long dresses were weaving towards me, arm in arm, laughing. They were, I guessed, fifteen or sixteen years old. They were hammered.

'Hey, mister!' They were shouting at me, I realised. 'Any chance of a ride?'

Ah, that chestnut. The two girls on the outside now grabbed the dress hem of their friend in the middle; for ones so drunk, they did this with incredible adroitness. They lifted her floaty skirt right up over her head and yanked at her knickers. Then I was past them and behind me I heard laughter and cries. 'You pervy scut,' someone said. And just then the street lights came on.

A moment later I passed the railings of Methody grammar, where I imagined some of those that I had brushed against that evening, maybe even the three girls I'd just passed, would be dropped off in the morning by their mothers or fathers, spruce in their uniforms, their hair combed and wet and tightly bound, their faces shiny, their uniforms clean and pressed, their bags packed, their finished homework within. It was dark here – at Methody's railings there was no street light – and it occurred to me I was probably the only person on the street who was alone, unaccompanied, and who had no intention of getting slaughtered later on. Then I emerged back into the light, the gossamer violet of dusk mixed with the yellowy light from the street lamps, and I went on, the sounds of revelry growing fainter with every step I took heading away from the city centre until, finally, I was so far gone, I couldn't hear the sounds any more.

WANKER
IAN
yo
yo
gerry ADAMS
we won

Finally, Finally, Finally (Wednesday, 31 August 1994)

When I got in to the office of the film production company where I work, I heard the television wittering in the kitchen. It was on so early because it was rumoured the IRA were about to announce a ceasefire. Inevitably, as the morning ran on, I found myself checking the TV regularly. So did everybody else in the office.

At some point, sensing it was coming – its nearness was in the air, crackling like static – everyone left their desks, went to the kitchen and huddled round the set, and not long after, it was announced: the ceasefire would start at midnight. Nobody said much. We trickled back to our desks.

And now, as is the way – this certainly amused the gods – today of all days, of all the days in Irish history, certainly late Irish history, the day the IRA declared a ceasefire, the day when I should be in Vincent's café on Botanic overhearing the barista and the customers bantering about the ceasefire, the day when I should be in Ormeau Park listening to sunbathers amiably chatting about the ceasefire, the day when I should be in the Crown bar at five eavesdropping on the after-work crowds bellowing to make themselves heard over the bar clamour as they shouted at one another about the ceasefire, today, of all days, when I already had one job working at the film production company, I'd agreed to take on another job: I'd agreed to do a colour piece for a magazine about Lord Charlemont's National Trust-owned summer house on Coney Island in the middle of Lough Neagh, forty miles from Belfast, and the English couple who were the caretakers. Definitely wrong place, wrong day.

I'd arranged a taxi to take me. The office doorbell rang and down to the street I went. The car stood at the kerb, a black Audi. I got into the front seat. The taximan, a beefy type in a short-sleeved shirt, turned up the radio and eased out into the traffic. The ubiquitous pine freshener dangling from the rear-view mirror swayed as we moved, and from the speaker came the voice of John Hume: his message (the IRA ending violence would facilitate a new political settlement for the whole of Ireland and this settlement should earn the allegiance of all traditions) was delivered in Hume's trademark plain, patient, dogged monotone. But then, having had to repeat the bleeding obvious for decades (Hume had always been right), was it any wonder he talked in the slightly hectoring schoolmasterly way he did?

The driver, listening as I was, tutted and shook his head. My eyes flicked to his bare forearms. I sensed he was a loyalist but couldn't be sure and I wondered if there were any giveaway tattoos – 'No Surrender', for instance, or the acronyms of any number of paramilitary organisations, all with 'U' for Ulster in them. But no, nothing.

The car's two-way radio barked into life.

Ah, I thought, his name might be a help – but it turned out to be Andy, which was no good to me either, being one of those irritating ones that both traditions used.

The taximan took the handset and spoke into it, and as he did so I looked at his face in profile. This is what you do when you're really stumped. You look at a face and hazard a guess. Of course, it's pointless. There's no such thing as a Catholic or a Protestant, a republican or a loyalist, face, except, well, sometimes … *Loyalist*, I thought. *Has to be.*

The taximan set the hand piece back in its holder and cleared his throat. *Here goes*, I thought.

'What do you think of all this peace thing?' he asked.

He aimed to sound neutral but he couldn't disguise an undercurrent of dismay mixed with truculence. Yep, I thought, any other day he'd be quiet but today, with the news reports and whatnot, he just wouldn't be able to stop himself. He had to blurt. The sluice gate had been lifted, the torrent was coming …

'I'm British,' he said, 'and there's a million more like me, and we don't like the sound of it –' he waved at the radio, so I'd be in no doubt that it was what John Hume had just said that had catalysed this outburst '– and we're not changing.'

He then explained, bluntly, frankly, charmlessly (the tone masking a small scintilla of anxiety as to my reaction) that he was a committed loyalist and an ex-prisoner.

'Ah,' I said, in the most encouraging manner I could manage. 'Tell me the story. What happened to you?' I had no anxiety about asking because I knew he would not have said he had been a prisoner unless he wanted to talk and tell all. And talk he now did, tumbling out his whole life story for me, baldly and without apology. The bare bones were these.

He grew up on a loyalist estate. His parents were decent, God-fearing, and from early childhood, the taximan, because of how he was reared, was quite clear in his own mind that ordinary, decent crime, like theft, was unconscionable. He never had and he never would steal – not even an apple from a greengrocer's shop.

However, what he also knew from childhood was that in Northern Ireland there was another category of behaviour underpinned by an ideology that, though some called it 'criminal', was in fact the very opposite of criminal: it was patriotic and sprang from the love of one's people and the love of one's state and the love of one's monarch.

And what exactly, I asked, was he talking about. (I knew the answer but I decided it would be better to pretend otherwise.)

Loyalism, of course. Show him a bad boy, he said – by which, he explained, he meant a hard-line republican – and, as a loyalist, he wouldn't shrink from 'doing' him.

'Meaning killing him?' I asked.

'If necessary, yes.'

But 'doing' a bad boy, he repeated, wasn't a crime; it was patriotism. Unfortunately, the British state didn't see that. And because of what he'd done to a bad boy, he'd got twelve years. 'It wasn't murder,' he added. He didn't go on to specify the exact nature of what he had done, but I did find myself thinking, *Hmm, a typical life sentence for murder is eleven and he got twelve. It wasn't murder, he said, so what did he do to get a higher tariff that one might usually get for killing someone? You don't get twelve years just for being the lookout or driving the getaway car … So what was he convicted of? Conspiracy to kill, weapons possession, manufacturing bombs …?*

'How was prison?' I asked. Conversationally speaking, that was the only place to go.

'Prison was wonderful,' he said.

'You don't meet a better class of person than you meet in the prison,' he continued, and he rhapsodised about the loyalist men he had met there. He'd been in the Maze in a segregated H-Block, so he'd only associated with paramilitaries who were in the same organisation as he was. Bliss …

'I'm out now, of course, but I haven't abandoned or forgotten my comrades,' he continued. 'I visit the Maze every week. And, what's more, now I am out, I only associate with ex-prisoners.'

'Oh,' I said, 'why?'

Prison had changed him. It had made him serious, careful, a new man all told. And this new man didn't want to waste time with trivial, boring and uninteresting people, which meant pretty much anyone who hadn't been in prison. Thus, his friendship group now consisted exclusively of loyalist ex-prisoners. His wife, he added, understood, accepted and supported his new lifestyle.

'Really?'

Yes. In fact he was going to a benefit, he continued, on Saturday coming, for a loyalist murdered by the IRA, and she was going with him; however, and this was what he wanted me to know, at the actual event he wouldn't be sitting with her. She'd be with the wives. And him? Well, he wouldn't be sitting with civilians, by which he meant everyone who hadn't been to prison. No. He'd be with the ex-prisoners.

'Really looking forward to Saturday night,' he said. 'Ex-prisoners never talk bullshit, like everyone else does.'

'Of course not.'

'And if they don't have anything to say, do you know what they do?'

'Tell me,' I said.

'They sit in silence. That's something you learn in jail – how to sit quietly with a man, not talking but not embarrassed, and when you come out you can still do it with men who've been in jail. We have this bond, you see, because of what we've been through. You know what I mean?'

Did I dare risk it? Why not? 'I think it's what the Buddha preaches,' I said. 'We must learn to sit still.'

He made no response to this – I don't think he took it in; he couldn't because his absolute commitment now was to tell me about Saturday night, and his words were coming thick and fast. The club where the function for the dead loyalist was being held would be full of muppets, he said, singing party songs and blathering about sticking it to the Fenians. 'Course they wouldn't have ever touched a gun in their lives, them ones. Chocolate soldiers, the lot of them. 'But here's the thing,' he continued, breathlessly, ecstatically, 'ex-prisoners, we know better than to waste time talking shite. We've done our bit. We don't need to rattle our sabres. That's another part of the prison effect. It wises a man up. Teaches him to wind his neck in and keep his gob shut.'

Ah. I nodded sagely. Was this going where I thought it was going? Was he implying the non-chocolate soldiers of his ilk were still prepared, unlike the fakes, the civilians, to do their bit and take the war to the republicans, even though they'd already done their whack? There was only one way to find out. Ask.

'And, ah –' the last thing I wanted was to come over as belligerent or quarrelsome or truculent, so I kept my voice soft, neutral and innocent '– would you, if push came to shove, go back to war?'

'Well,' he said. His tone was different too; he had something important to say but he was going to say it carefully. 'The wife and cubs,' he said, 'are my priorities now. I wouldn't do anything to jeopardise them. But my beliefs haven't changed. I oppose a united Ireland and the Dublin government, one hundred and ten per cent.'

'One hundred and ten per cent?'

'Yeah.'

'And that will never change?'

'Never.'

'And the ceasefire?'

He shook his head, smiled. It was a smile that said, *No way, mate.* He wouldn't be shifting any time soon and nor, I guessed, would his fellow ex-loyalist prisoners. The place where he lived might be about to undergo change but not him, not his cohort. He and they, they had their principles and, nope, they weren't for turning, they weren't bending, they weren't for going green. So in other words, when it came to violence, it wasn't never again, but rather, never say never.

We left the motorway and followed a lattice-like mesh of country roads to a marina. A drake and a mallard were asleep in the middle of the car park we drove into. As we approached they did not move. I liked that, their implacability. The sun was out, and when it was, this was where they slept and they weren't moving. The indifference of the natural world is always enlightening, always a corrective in febrile political times. We are not the only living things on this planet; there are others, and their preoccupations are quite different to ours.

The taximan scooted around the ducks and parked and I got out and there they were, the caretakers, an English couple from the Lake District, Mel and Julia Dowding, in a boat by the quayside. The lake shimmered like tinfoil. I heard the harsh piping cries of waterbirds and smelt the dank smell of brackish inland water.

I climbed aboard the Dowdings' boat; introductions made, we puttered away. Behind, on the shore, I saw an old stone tower; and now, facing forwards, a small wooded hump, an island straight out of Arthur Ransome's *Swallows and Amazons*. Coney Island … a heron in the reeds, grey and austere, and, somewhere behind, another old stone tower ...

Next, inevitably, the history lesson. The tower on the island, my host and hostess said, was an O'Neill tower, and the tower on the shore an O'Connor tower. Once upon a time the Gaelic O'Neills and O'Connors faced one another here from their separate strongholds. Then came the seventeenth-century plantation, the year zero in Ulster history, when their Gaelic order was swept aside and the new English or Elizabethan order was put in its place. The O'Neills' lands, Coney Island included, went to the Caulfield family, and the O'Connors' lands to some other planter. How often, I thought, and not for the first time, does one meet this moment in Ulster, this line that separates everything that was from everything that followed, everything pre-plantation being Old Testament, BC, Catholic and Irish, and everything post-plantation being New Testament, AD, Protestant and English, and depending on which side of the line one identified with, everything followed – politics, beliefs, religion, the whole kit and caboodle. The taximan knew he belonged on the plantation side of the line, whereas I, at least by birth, belonged to the pre-plantation side (though originating in a different part of Ireland). We all know our origin story – and worse, very often, so does everyone else.

At the island's jetty, a dog waited, snuffling and shaking with joy. We tied up and clambered ashore. The tower I'd seen was a tumble of old stone. Behind, a green lawn and flower beds and a house – built by a Caulfield descendant, Alfred, Lord Charlemont, in 1895 as a holiday home – where the Dowdings were now living.

It was a simple, unpretentious house, with lichen-covered roof tiles and green-painted sash windows. I followed my hosts through the front door and into the hall: gumboots and fishing rods and a huge blank wall with planks nailed over it.

'The Boy Scouts used to come here in the 1940s,' Mel explained, 'and there's a mural they did behind there, apparently not very good.'

'Naked women, knowing the Scouts,' his wife ventured.

'In that case,' said Mel, 'we'll have to have those planks off. Ba-boom.'

We sauntered through rooms filled with greenish light (the leaves on the trees outside were the cause), me listening, my hosts talking the home-improvement talk new householders relish – our topics included a Rayburn that leaked tar, the Dowdings' first Christmas on the island, the colours on the walls in the rooms and the difficulties of choosing paints that matched. It was a perfect conversation for the purposes of the article I had to write, with Mel and Julia's story being just the sort of story I was supposed to garner: lovely couple leading a lovely life in a lovely house in – and here was the clincher, the real USP – Northern Ireland.

Oh yes, that was exactly what the readers of the glossy magazine I was working for would happily pay to read – a nice, happy, uplifting good-news colour story, with no nastiness, no paramilitaries, no gore, no Ulster malarkey, just good, honest-to-God pro-consumer copy. At the same time, at the edge of my thoughts, I did notice that the irritation I'd felt earlier that I would be far from Belfast, where I believed I ought to be, today of all days, had been moved aside by the notion that there was something for me to learn here, and had I still been in the city I would not have been taught this – or re-taught this, to be really accurate. Northern Ireland was amalgam: on the one hand there was this happy, glowing English couple high on their great good fortune in having landed in Lord Charlemont's summer house on Coney Island, and on the other there was the taximan with his dour talk about the flinty integrity of ex-prisoners who might or might not go back to war and who wanted nothing to do with the ceasefire, and who was waiting for me on the quayside. This place was shade and light, insanity and geniality, obduracy and generosity; a dysfunctional basket case and somewhere rich with possibility. A very odd place indeed.

Back on the quayside, the taximan was sitting with the driver-side door open, staring at the clear blue sky. The radio was on. The ceasefire talk was still flowing. At the water's edge a group of boys, eleven or twelve years old, were puffing away, sending great clouds of blue smoke up into the summer air. I remembered a Lewis Hine photograph, *Newspaper Boys Smoking, St. Louis, Missouri*, and was obscurely delighted at the match – a contemporary moment and an old black-and-white.

I got in to the taxi. The taximan nodded, closed his door carefully, turned the key in the ignition and slowly drove away. He didn't say a word all the way to Belfast.

In the evening I made notes about my day. 'It's lovely the way they take it in turns to finish one another's lines,' I wrote about Mel and Julia. 'If only our leaders had this talent.'

Shortly before midnight I thought I heard gunfire. It came from the west of Belfast and it had a popping pantomime quality. I assumed these were republican guns, IRA guns, I was hearing, and they were declaring victory. If they were guns, that is. I wasn't sure. It might have been fireworks.

I got into bed: my little room was at the front of the flat, overlooking Eglantine Avenue, and as I lay waiting for sleep I listened to the intoxicated, staggering carousers who passed below my window, as they made their way home many of them singing. Now and again I heard party songs – 'The Sash My Father Wore' or 'The Men behind the Wire' – but mostly they were singing songs from musicals, with *Grease*, by a country mile, the favourite.

Pre-dawn, the phone rang. It went on ringing. It wouldn't stop. I got up and went to it – it was out in the front hall of the flat – and picked up the handset.

'Did you party in West Belfast last night?' I heard. It was my insomniac friend R.

'Do you know what time it is?' I said.

'Do you know what the IRA did last night?'

'Fired their guns into the air?'

'They went around all the police stations in West Belfast,' he said, 'and painted over the Royal Ulster Constabulary signs and wrote "Garda Síochána" beside them.'

'No, I did not know that,' I said

'The ceasefire's hardly started and this already,' he said. 'Years of pain, we're about to try peace, but these cunts want us to think they've won, for fuck's sake.'

He talked away and I laughed at his disparaging anti-Provo invective, unstinting, sharp, light and brutal. The laughing took away my tiredness. I perked up.

The call ended and as I knew I wouldn't get back to sleep I decided I'd go to work. I got dressed and set off on my bicycle. The light in the streets was filmy, the air mild. At the end of Camden Street, a knot of soldiers and policemen were standing and talking. I'd never before seen uniforms looking so relaxed. Did they know something I didn't? Did they think they were the winners? Or was this just relief that after decades this disgusting conflict (which was actually a civil war) was finally over? I was still wondering about this when I got to the building where the office was. I unlocked the front door and then went back for my bicycle, which I'd left on the pavement, and carried it inside.

★

The loyalists announced their ceasefire a few weeks later, on 13 October 1994.

IS
C WING PROTESTANT BOYS
LONG KESH
FLUTE BAND

Down with the Paramilitaries (Wednesday, 7 June 1995)

In Northern Ireland one part of the population very much wants to be British and the other doesn't, and one expression of that schism are the two names used for the prison where loyalist and republican paramilitary prisoners are housed. The explanation is as follows.

In 1971 internment was introduced, and the republican internees (who were not processed by a court but simply rounded up and bundled away) were put into compounds (Nissen huts, barbed-wire fences, very World War II). One of these sites, from 1972 on, was Long Kesh, an old airfield outside Belfast. Mid-seventies, a proper prison with iconic H-shaped blocks was built beside the compounds to house paramilitary prisoners who'd been sentenced in a court (a Diplock court, of course, from 1973 onwards, so no jury, just a judge) and which the authorities named Her Majesty's Prison Maze. Republicans, geniuses in the public relations department, immediately spotted what the Northern Ireland Office (and the British state) were up to with this new prison: they were signalling that Northern Ireland was leaving the disaster of internment (and the compounds) behind and moving to a new, improved, forward-looking phase. Naturally, the republicans were having no truck with this. Of course not. If they lost Long Kesh, internment would be forgotten and they wanted to keep internment, which had been such a gift to their argument, before the public eye. They refused to call the new jail the Maze prison and called it Long Kesh instead; after all, that's what the compounds beside which it stood were called, so why not, they pedantically opined. And so Long Kesh it was, and they never budged, and this brilliant act of linguistic disobedience, besides its propaganda value (when the hunger strikers died in 1981, they died not in HMP Maze but in Long Kesh, that byword for Albion's perfidiousness), had all sorts of unintended consequences, one of which I met at the start of my day.

I had no car in Belfast and I needed a lift to HMP Maze to do my day's work as a teacher of creative writing. The probation office in the prison are technically my employers so they arranged for Donald, a probation officer, to get me there. At the time agreed, he appeared outside my office in his car and in I got. How was he? I asked. He rolled his eyes.

'Republicans,' he began, 'order stuff from the Littlewoods catalogue by the ton, and what do they give as the return address?'

'Don't know. Buckingham Place?'

'Ha, ha. Long Kesh! Which isn't where they are and doesn't have a postcode anyhow. Then they complain because their orders don't come ...'

And so, he continued, the day before he'd had to call Littlewoods to sort out a mountain of missing prisoner orders, and as usual it had been a bizarre and exhausting experience, with the Littlewoods person repeatedly telling him he should tell the republicans to use the right name plus the postcode or else. He acted the scene.

Donald: 'What, you're saying, go on the wings and lay down the law?'

Littlewoods person: 'Absolutely!'

Donald: 'You do know the republicans aren't good at taking suggestions.'

Littlewoods person: 'What! You're in charge, they're prisoners. You *make* them do what you want.'

Donald: 'Well, they tried that with hunger strikes and look how well that turned out?'

The woman at Littlewoods had no idea what he was talking about. 'A perfect example of the ignorance of the English when it comes to this place,' Donald said.

He ought to have found her lack of knowledge funny, he added, but he couldn't. He found it exasperating, infuriating and depressing, and it had taken a whole evening of Schubert before he'd felt half-normal again.

Inside the Maze, Donald was my escort; I hadn't got my full pass yet, the one that would allow me to move around alone. Our first destination was H2, home to the Ulster Defence Association (UDA) loyalist cohort, and after a good walk (the prison estate is enormous), the block came into view. H2 was a long, low ugly structure, with wires with dangling orange balls strung everywhere (to deter helicopters landing) and enormously tall poles around the edges with night lights at the top. Taken together, everything screamed 'penal' (you couldn't be anywhere except a prison), only not traditional penal, nineteenth-century Victorian panoptical penal, nice, cosy penal, like in *Porridge* with lovable Ronnie Barker playing genial old lag Norman Fletcher. No, what the structure screamed was twentieth-century penal, gulag penal, hardcore penal, 'Don't mess with us, you little paramilitary fucker. We're harder than you and don't you forget it, pal!' penal.

When we got to the door in the middle of the cross strut connecting the two uprights of the H where the cells are, Donald stopped. He looked slightly anxious.

'You'd better steel yourself,' he said. 'There might be a bit of friction.'

'Oh?'

'The ones who did Greysteel have just landed here,' he explained.

Greysteel is a small village on the coast near Derry. On Saturday, 30 October 1993, three members of the UDA, Stephen Irwin, Geoffrey Deeney and Torrens Knight, entered the Rising Sun Bar – a Halloween party was underway and about seventy guests were in attendance – and opened fire, killing eight and wounding nineteen. I'd seen photographs of the trio. I had been particularly struck by the photograph of Torrens Knight in suit and tie, short-haired, a Remembrance Sunday poppy in his lapel, shouting with such rage as he was led to or from court by two RUC constables that the cords of his neck stood out. He was anger in the raw, rage personified and completely unregulated.

'They're a bit immature,' Donald continued.

'Oh.'

'And they've fallen out with Michael Stone.'

Michael Stone was a UDA member (and legend in loyalist circles) who had been convicted of three counts of murder, including the Milltown Cemetery attack, and thirteen later charges, including five counts of attempted murder.

'On account of this mural he's done,' said Donald. 'It's got this very Sinn Féin dove, with a very Sinn Féin message below: "Consolidate the peace".'

No, anything remotely Sinn Féiny was obviously not going to chime with Knight or his co-defendants. I got that.

We went through the front door, Donald and I, and into H2. There was a pod with an officer and Donald handed him my pass. The toilets were behind – the whisper of a gushing cistern and the smell of disinfectant balls bobbing in urinals. Directly ahead was the crossbar of the H that connected the two uprights, with the gate, or grille, in the middle. I said goodbye to Donald and went on through. I was now in a world without officers as staff aren't often on the landings any more, much to the outrage of politicians and policemen and the Prison Officers Association, who argue that this no-touch regime, as it is sometimes waggishly called, is a reward by the state to criminals for bad behaviour.

I made my way rightwards past the mural, which was, as reported, very Sinn Féiny, towards a wing from which I could hear mute sounds drifting: the susurrus of male voices, thumping music, the squeak of rubber-soled shoes on buffered linoleum, flip-flops flopping …

I stepped onto the wing and crossed and went into a space that was both dinner hall and kitchen. Stainless steel shining dully. A faint reek of cabbage and batter. The smell of Brillo, scoured metal and sour carbolic. There were prisoners dotted about, sitting and standing, having breakfast. I smelt toast and the metal tang of industrial tinned marmalade. The smell of milk and of men in the morning, the peculiar male odour that I first met in dormitories in Bedales School as a boarder in the 1960s. I muttered 'Good morning' and nodded, but nothing came back from this prisoner with his prison bowl of prison cornflakes and that one with his prison mug of prison tea. I wondered if these were the Greysteel ones, but I couldn't connect the images from the papers with the men I saw now. *Maybe not*, I thought. Actually, probably not. These men I was passing were old hands; they had been here years; they were bedded in. They weren't newbies. I was sure of it.

I moved on, and as I went I tried to assess their mood. They weren't hostile, just indifferent and bored and ever-so-slightly surly: the male default when all else fails. *Do they know I'm the man who teaches creative writing?* I wondered. Had they seen me coming in and out before? Maybe not, but they would at least know there was someone like me floating about, I reasoned. They must have been informed by their Officer Commanding (OC) that I was teaching, surely? I hoped so but I didn't know and that, of course, made it impossible to muffle the little threads of anxiety I could feel stirring. The fact was, I was a wayfarer, an interloper, and I was there on sufferance. Whatever assurances I offered myself, this was a foreign land with customs and rules and protocols I did not understand. I was an alien.

I opened the door I'd been heading for and stepped into the classroom-cum-store where I taught in H2. Though it was actually a square airless space in a modern concrete and steel prison, one that boasted it was the most secure in Europe, the room felt like an ancient attic. There were chairs and tables, one-gallon plastic industrial containers filled with green disinfectant, a mop and a pail, kitchen utensils and, piled everywhere, Orange Order paraphernalia, which went up on the landings when the loyalist prisoners celebrated the Twelfth, the victory at the Battle of the Boyne: banners with King Billy astride his rearing charger and Orange arches listing Northern Ireland's six counties. There were also fat Lambeg drums, bandsmen's hats and bandsmen's gloves and even bandsmen's pace sticks. Everything here was made with materials scavenged in the prison – cardboard and old tins, polystyrene and coat hangers, blanket patches and rope short ends. As I looked around I remembered the tin toys from Soweto – beautifully fabricated model cars made from coloured tin cans stamped with pictures of pilchards and tomatoes – that I used to see in Portobello Road market when I lived in London, and feeling when I saw them exactly what I was now feeling here in the Maze: the excitement that arises from direct contact with human ingenuity, the ability to conjure something out of almost nothing, which in turn reminded me of the curious fact that a copy of an industrially produced ideal will always stir me more than its better-made doppelganger. A handmade prison Lambeg is more moving than a factory-made one.

I rearranged the chairs for the class; I was expecting four or five. The little threads of anxiety I had felt in the kitchen were still there, still weaving faintly through my guts, and were now overlaid with a new anxiety. The room I was now in was a room off a room. God forbid if anything went wrong: it was a long way to the grille that separated me from the front circle and the closest officer in the pod in the entrance hall. But we were where we were, as the platitude went. And if I didn't want to do this, I shouldn't do it, and of course I did want to. Oh yes. And why was that?

It was greed, of course – not material greed (though I was being paid to do this by the Northern Ireland Office, I presumed, even though it was the Probation Board who issued the cheques) but another kind of greed: my insatiable, ravenous appetite to meet with, talk to and hear from the people who lived where I lived but whose values were utterly at odds with mine. I was here, and willing to endure the anxieties that threaded my gut, for the bedrock reason that I had to know.

My class filed in. Five, as expected. Michael Stone, the muralist, assured me he'd been writing, but not for me. He'd been writing press releases for the UDA, being now its official press officer. The IRA and Sinn Féin had been writing proper press releases for years, he explained, and now the loyalists were catching up. 'What took you so long?' one of the others class members asked. 'We're slow learners,' came Stone's answer. Not exactly friendly. More a response that signalled, *I can take some slagging but don't push it.* Stone turned to me. He intended to continue what he had started. When it came to the writing of press releases, Stone said, they really had caught up with the other side. They'd looked at the republicans and they'd learnt how important the written word was. And that was why I was there, he added: to teach them, to help them to be better communicators and better writers. I agreed. I was.

It was unexpected and odd for me to think I was putting my shoulder to their wheel. I wasn't a loyalist and I didn't see the world as loyalists saw it. But there I was, doing what I did. And I wasn't a republican either, yet when I was working with them I was doing the same – putting my shoulder to their wheel. And I was aware many disapproved. In the Maze, several officers had waylaid me and told me, politely, jocularly but never shyly, that I shouldn't be doing the teaching I was doing because of the nature of the people I was teaching. I had no answer to the second half of their objection. They were right. The people I was teaching had done terrible things. But I had an answer to the first part of their sentence and it was that I wasn't going to not teach. So when accosted, I always gave the same answer. 'Yes,' I said, my tone suitably rueful, 'teaching's a dirty job, but someone's got to do it …'

I gave a little talk to my class – I always had a little literary talk prepared; this one was on the way writers use themselves, or versions of themselves, in their fiction. Obviously, I was trying to encourage the class to write honestly yet slantwise about their lives by fictionalising themselves. The examples I used (all literary texts, which I guessed might be unfamiliar, and I wanted to take them right away from the familiar) were Robert Westall's *Falling into Glory*, Esther Freud's *Hideous Kinky*, Alain-Fournier's *Le Grand Meaulnes* and Rudyard Kipling's *Plain Tales from the Hills*. I also mentioned how V. S. Naipaul put himself into his magisterial, majestic and highly offensive travel book *India: A Million Mutinies Now*.

Then we went to work. The men read what they'd written and we discussed it. Last order of the morning was the play M. had written, and we read it aloud, each of us taking a role. We got so carried away we found ourselves standing up and moving around as if we were in rehearsal. The play's plot was as follows.

An Ulster town is on its last legs economically because the main employer, a fairground, has closed down. Two friends, one a Catholic, the other a Protestant (but neither extreme, nor with paramilitary connections), hatch a plan: they'll sell a fake UFO story to the tabloids and use the proceeds to buy the funfair. The lads get to work and succeed – they make a lot of money with their invented story – but then the Catholic begins to have doubts. He was never employed at the fairground. Catholics aren't. They've always been second-class citizens in their own country. This revelation coming to the character is irrefutable. He decides he won't contribute to save the fairground, and Northern Ireland, the play implies, is similarly doomed because our two traditions, following the miserable manner in which the majority have persecuted and denigrated and humiliated the minority, never can and never will pull together.

The play's style was broad and comic, and the writer was clearly influenced by British television soaps and sitcoms. But the play's assertion – the historical wrongs done to the minority were so egregious reconciliation was impossible – was an idea I doubted one would ever see on British television in a soap or a sitcom. And how interesting, I thought, that I should collide with this level of bracing pessimism (the problem of Northern Ireland, its baked-in sectarianism, was unsolvable) on a UDA wing. *This place is full of surprises.*

In the kitchen, next door, I heard the sound of the Dixie lids clanging and plates banging and ladles scraping. The midday meal was approaching. We agreed to reconvene at the same time the following week, the class and I, and I said goodbye. Then I slid through the door and into the dinner-hall-cum-kitchen – steaming pots and hissing gas jets. A couple of orderlies, who at first glance appeared to be wearing long gloves like those sported by ladies at Viennese balls but which on closer inspection turned out to be sleeves of tattoos, were preparing the midday meal. They watched me as I went past but offered neither greeting nor acknowledgement. On the far side of the kitchen, I stepped through to the wing, where I instinctively looked down to my right. Every cell stood open, the doors with their prominent Judas slits mostly sitting in the recesses in the wall constructed to hold them, although one or two stuck out a bit, like tongues. Here was a photograph: a set of openings, through which entry into the mysterious interior of each cell was made, receding uniformly all the way to the bottom. It had graphic power but also narrative heft, as it contained in itself the revelation of the future to come: at some point the prisoners would return and each would go into his cell and each cell door would then be swung shut and the cell would swallow its occupant for the night. Yes, the prisoners ran the wing and they organised their own cooking and they had very little interaction with the officers, day to day, et cetera, et cetera. It looked like they had it cushy. But every night they slept in their cells between cold walls, and no matter how much they augmented and personalised the spaces with pictures and posters and photographs and nice duvet covers and so on, it could never ever be anything other than a cell. Oh yes, this was jail. Fact. Not jail as most people knew it, but nonetheless still jail.

I got out onto the crossbar where the mural was and went through the grille to the hallway beyond, where Donald was waiting for me. We left the block and started to walk. An Irish summer's day. Mild and damp. Sense of relief to be out. When I am behind bars, even though I know intellectually I will eventually leave, my muscles and my nervous system aren't quite so sure. I feel anxious or constrained or incarcerated, and as soon as I am free there is a tingling surge of energy that comes with release. I felt that now.

Donald and I walked past fences and H-Blocks to the Portakabin that housed the probation office and where the probation officers ate. I had brought sandwiches. The room was dark after the bright outside – chairs and armchairs and low tables and probation officers sitting around; the smell of cheddar and Branston Pickle and sliced white pan. The same atmosphere as a school staffroom. In front of a low table sat a woman who looked a good deal older than everyone else. She was slight and slender and wore bright-red lipstick that glowed hypnotically in the gloomy interior. I had seen her once before, outside, in a bookshop. It was Helen Lewis.

Born in Trutnov, in German-speaking Sudetenland in Czechoslovakia, she'd trained as a dancer at the Milča Mayerová school of dance in Prague. She married in 1938, and in 1942 she was deported together with her husband, Paul, to Terezín, the Jewish ghetto, and then to Auschwitz, where she and her husband were separated. After liberation she returned to Prague where she discovered her husband had not survived. In 1947 she married Harry, an old friend who had escaped to Belfast before the start of the war, and moved to Northern Ireland, where she lived and worked and raised a family.

We were introduced, shook hands; I sat and we began to talk about our mornings. She had been with the republicans.

'And look,' she said, 'how nice, they have given me this book.' Her voice was the lovely, fruity, rich Mitteleuropean voice I used to hear in certain cafés when I lived in London.

Helen turned the book towards me on the table to show me what it was: an anthology of republican writing about the hunger strikes called *Nor Meekly Serve My Time: The H-Block Struggle, 1976–1981.*

'And not only have they given me this,' she said, 'but also, they have signed it.'

Helen began to turn the pages. I saw a blur of different names, some in English, some in Irish.

'Some names at the front,' she said. 'And some inside, and everyone – everyone – has signed.'

'Yep, every single man in the block has signed it,' a probation officer chipped in.

Helen went on turning the pages. Ah yes, I thought, as they flickered past, here was a classic example of republican practice – and proof, if needed, that they had no truck, like the loyalists, with the idea that it was every man's right to think what he wanted but were, on the contrary a tight, disciplined, single-minded revolutionary organisation whose membership acted in concert. Typically, books get signed by their makers, their writers or editors, but with *Nor Meekly Serve My Time* it was everyone, not just contributors. And for what reason had people scrawled their names even if they hadn't directly had anything to do with the book? Because in the republican world they had. In the republican world it wasn't individuals who made the book: in the republican world it was the movement that had made it; therefore, every volunteer had played his part, so therefore, every volunteer in the movement must sign regardless.

Helen closed the book. 'I got them to write their questions down in advance,' she said.

She had a heap of pink slips in front of her. 'A lot of questions,' she said, 'as you can see.'

She rummaged through the slips and found one. 'You will like this one,' she said. 'Why did the British not honour their agreement with Czechoslovakia after Munich in 1938?' Her eyes twinkled. 'A little bit of bias there, as I expected, of course.'

After we'd finished eating, we got out of everyone's earshot. She was returning to the republicans in the afternoon with the pink slips to answer more questions. How did I find them, she wondered. What was my first encounter like, for instance? This was a question I had to answer.

My first time on a republican landing, I said, I was shown to the classroom and told to wait. My class would be along presently. I was left alone, which with hindsight I saw was planned. There was a mural on the wall, almost life-size. A Belfast terraced house, a man at the front door with a sledgehammer raised – he was clearly going to break the door down – and three men behind him with Armalite rifles, ready to rush in. All four wore balaclavas. My class arrived, along with a man who styled himself the OC. I didn't catch of what. 'What's behind the door?' I asked, pointing at the mural. 'The man they're going to kill,' said the OC, blithely. He introduced himself as Fermanagh born and bred. 'Very good,' I said. He mentioned the schoolhouse where I lived and the chapel beside the schoolhouse where, he said, he'd attended Mass. Small world, he said, him going to the chapel beside the house where I lived. I nodded. He mentioned the Integrated School. He approved. Educating Catholics and Protestants together was the only way to go, wasn't it? I agreed. It was. That was exactly what he expected me to say, he said. After all, weren't my children at the Integrated School? His talk meandered on. He knew so many people I knew. He named them. And so many people who knew my wife too. He named them too. Small place, County Fermanagh, he said. Small town, Enniskillen, he said. Everyone knew everyone else's business. It was suffocating, he said dreamily, but at the same time everyone looked out for everyone else and wasn't that the point of a small place and wasn't that rather wonderful? I agreed and he said he was pleased I understood him. (Of course I did. I couldn't have failed to catch his drift.) Now we can move on to housekeeping, he said. I was not to engage anyone about their feelings, morals or offences, and if I did the class had been instructed to get up and walk out. Did I understand? I did, and as I said this I wondered if I should tell him the loyalists had no such rules. I doubted he'd want to hear that, so I didn't. Well, that's great, he said. He'd go and I could begin. He toddled off.

The republicans, I said to Helen at the end of my account, were tight and disciplined in a way the loyalists weren't. Every republican sang from the same hymn sheet. In her reply, which linked this conversation back to the book *Nor Meekly Serve My Time* that so many IRA men had signed, Helen observed how like Stalinists the republicans were – although, she added, the Catholic Church and believing Catholics might be the better comparison for them.

In the afternoon I walked to H3 with Donald. H3 was the block where I'd taught my first-ever class in the Maze (this was on the morning of the same day I'd first taught republicans, which had been in the afternoon) and that memorable class – the one with the loyalists – had nearly not happened for reasons that had gradually been revealed to me over the proceeding months.

Two days before I was due to teach my first class in H3, an officer in another loyalist block had spotted a prisoner in the yard speaking on a mobile phone. The officer demanded the phone; the prisoner refused to hand it over. If you have a phone in jail, of course you're going to keep it. The two fought and the officer prevailed. The prison authorities then decided to search *all* the loyalist wings for mobile phones. As the search team (sometimes referred to as the riot squad) was being rostered and dispatched, H3 were warned that a search team was coming to do a full cell search. The loyalist prisoners in H3 decided that would not happen.

When the search team arrived, the prisoners in H3 set everything flammable on fire; they threw their burning bedding and mattresses into the yard but left the furniture to burn in situ. The fire alarms tripped (their monotonous, moronic din accompanied the battle that followed) and terrible toxic black smoke filled the building and poured out the windows. The search team donned their fire hazard suits and their breathing gear and turned on the fire hoses. They fired in the pressurised streams, flooding the block with water, which quickly turned black. The prisoners got onto the roof and, using home-made catapults, fired billiard balls coated in highly inflammable Evo-Stik glue through a hole in the roof into the control room (the brains of the block). The Evo-Stik was supposed to attach the burning billiard balls like burrs to the officers' clothes and set them alight.

Meanwhile, inside the block, barricades went up as the search team pushed in, beating their batons on their shields, just like Roman centurions did (at least in the movies) when marching towards the barbarians they were about to destroy in battle. On the landings, hand-to-hand fighting, the officers using their batons and shields, the prisoners using pool cues, table legs, planks and anything else they could lay their hands on. The air was filled with noxious smoke and it was difficult to see; the floor was awash with dirty water and it was hard not to slip. The fighting was nasty, vicious, prolonged, dangerous ... Eventually, inevitably, the search team prevailed and subdued the prisoners, but it took a day. That was the account I got, and I didn't doubt someone on the other side, the staff side, would have given a rather different version. Everything here in the prison is contested and every event has two sides, each completely at odds with the other.

My class being imminent, it was mooted whether it should go ahead. The block was wrecked, charred, sodden. The prisoners in H3 convened a meeting and Billy Giles, who believed passionately in education, argued strongly that the class must go ahead. He prevailed. When I'd showed up there were mounds of burnt detritus piled in the yard, the walls were black, and the air was rank with the stink of fetid water and scorch and burn. And now, today, which was months later, the stink lingered. The pod inside was still under repair; the officer who took one's pass was in a Portakabin parked outside in the yard. Donald had handed in his pass along with mine – he was going to sit in on this class – and together we went in.

The classroom was bare and there was a smell of disinfectant, which I think had been laid down to mask the charred smell. The class consisted of Billy Giles (thin, blue-eyed, 37); P., an older man with a cross and ring on a chain around his neck who had difficulties speaking owing to a stroke; N., who wore big earrings and tinted John Lennon spectacles; and D., blond, Teutonic-looking, quiet, a listener.

Billy Giles offered to speak first. He'd written a letter that he was going to use as the basis for a play set in the prison censor's office. His lead character, the prison-officer-cum-censor, is a Paisleyite bigot who has all the usual prejudices (he doesn't like homosexuals, he thinks young offenders should be flogged, and so forth). I thought the idea was excellent (I'd love to see a play set in a prison censor's office), but the censor character was a standard-issue baddie, I said. If he was simply awful all the way through, why would we watch? Only a change in his character (of some sort, either for better or for worse) would guarantee the interest of anyone watching, I said.

P. had written a piece of memoir about prison life for his grandson. It was full of Maze banter and nicely skewered the incongruities of prison life.

N. had written a poem which celebrated the stars and natural world. 'It all came about,' he said, pointing at the lights in the yard, which we could see through the barred windows, 'because with the haze that comes when the security lights are on at night, you can't see the stars. Anyway, after we rioted' – he meant the riot just before I'd started – 'I was beaten, so was everyone, and after they were done I was trussed up like a turkey by a couple of goons and trailed out to the yard. Though it was very early in the morning the security lights were off, and I couldn't stop staring up at the beautiful dawn sky with a few pale stars scattered over it in absolute amazement, and the goons were like, "What are you looking at?" and I said, "That beautiful sky …"'

'You don't see the sky in here,' said Billy Giles, 'and you have no sense, really, of the seasons or the weather. Imprisonment separates you from the natural world, you know. But that's something you wouldn't understand till you come to prison.'

We all turned to look out the window. Through the bars we could see the orange balls strung across the yard. The wind blew and the wires swayed and the balls jiggled.

'You know what the Provvies said when they saw them orange balls?' asked N.

'No,' I said.

'There's a sight for sore eyes, so many orange balls strung up.'

N.'s next poem was called 'Reports Are Coming In'. 'Reports are coming in' is the catchphrase of Eamonn Mallie, the local political journalist on Downtown Radio, who often interrupts his broadcasts with the words, 'Reports are coming in …'

N.'s poem, a ballad about intercommunal sectarian violence, ended with the gleeful anticipation among loyalists of reports coming in of another dead republican.

To me this came over as gloating. Now, the question was, did I air my views or not? N. might take the point or he might not. A disagreement at this stage might change the dynamics of the moment; maybe it was better to let this bad poem pass for now and hope that a chance to return to it in a subtle, non-confrontational way might arise a bit later. I decided to risk it. I asked N. to read another poem. He did. It was called 'Why?' It was about his cousin who'd died of solvent abuse.

'When I heard the news my cousin had died,' he said when he finished – the news of his cousin's death had catalysed the poem – 'I thought, *Why wasn't it me who died?* Why didn't I die because of what I had done, you know, just killed people, ruined people's lives. Why wasn't I called away?'

This was a surprise after the previous poem.

'Of course, it was very selfish to write it,' N. continued, 'pouring my problems out onto the page.'

'Why?'

'Well, in jail you can't show you're upset,' he said, 'in case you bring someone else down.'

'Really? Who says?'

'No one, it's just the way it is. Grief, despair, you know, you bottle it. You never let it show in case you infect some other man and make him sick with yours.'

'Ah.'

'Anyhow,' continued N., 'do you think anyone will want to read this stuff in years to come, apart from those who've lived here? I mean, it's an unfashionable war, isn't it?'

There was my door, the one I'd been waiting for. 'No one wants to read propaganda or gloating rhetoric,' I said. 'But writing which comes from the heart, like your last poem, will be read in a hundred years.'

Everyone in the room knew what I meant. It was the previous poem I was really speaking about. But I had come at the point indirectly, obliquely. Perseus couldn't face the Medusa front on; he had to use a mirror when he severed her head. We often have to avoid the frontal and go sideways.

The class ended. As the men shuffled out, Donald whispered, 'You earned your money's worth this afternoon.'

I wasn't so sure about that. I had just been lucky.

As we made our way back to the circle, he said, 'Jeepers, they're absolutely obsessed with the idea of doing their whack, aren't they?'

I didn't disagree.

On the way home in the car, Donald turned to sport. 'I follow a bit of rugby,' he said, 'and the team were playing in Limerick last week and you know what? They played "The Soldier's Song" before the match. Arseholes! If they came up to the north we wouldn't play "The Queen". We have more sense than to do that. Plus, we know that if we did there'd be outrage, cries of "unionist triumphalism" and coat-trailing and what have you. But down south they see absolutely nothing wrong in doing the very thing they'd hate if it was done to them. Wankers.'

As he dropped me off, Donald said, 'See you tomorrow.' The following day I was back in the Maze with the republicans.

★

What shocked me when I started working with paramilitaries was that none of them, bar the occasional loyalist, expressed regret or contrition. The only things they seemed to be sorry about were that they'd been caught, and some, I sensed, were even sorry they hadn't killed more people. But then I acclimatised (this happened remarkably speedily) and the shock receded. And I rationalised: of course, they weren't regretful or contrite. They belonged to revolutionary organisations committed to the use of violence to achieve their aims. In their eyes, the end (a United Ireland, or Keeping Ulster British, take your pick) justified the means (killing, bombing, torturing, tarring, maiming, beating, punishing and the rest).

Once I'd arrived at this understanding, I was able to agree a set of principles with myself:

- *Outside the prison's walls I interacted with people whose beliefs were alien to me and who doubtless found my beliefs alien to them. And for the most part things worked out because of the unspoken agreement, to which we all subscribe, to avoid disagreement. In the H-Blocks, there was no reason why that same understanding couldn't apply. We could all just agree to disagree. Or to say nothing and leave it at that.*
- *Feelings remained, however, and had to be managed. I couldn't pretend I wasn't troubled. Therefore, in order to teach, detachment was necessary and had to be consciously cultivated.*
- *I always needed to remember what I was doing: I was just there to instruct. I wasn't there to change or persuade, and indeed, had it been suspected that I was, I doubt I'd have lasted.*

Did I make progress having adopted these principles? I'd like to say I did. Work was certainly produced. But one insuperable difficulty remained. Whenever I professed that a writer's development was in direct ratio to their self-knowledge deepening, and that the more writers knew and accepted about themselves the further writers would go, I always got pushback. The men didn't like such talk. I believed they feared I was trying to open them up to contrition and their resistance left me wondering if furthering self-knowledge was put on hold in prison as a coping strategy.

It was only much later that I learnt how wrong I was and that almost every prisoner I interacted with of whatever stripe or kind was secretly engaged in the business of getting to the bottom of him or herself (I taught women later). In prison, every prisoner was obliged to spend time with the last person they ever expected to have to spend time with – namely, themselves, and in the dark hours of the night, in the solitude of a small cell, lying on a thin mattress, the white light from the security lights outside slanting across the face, when sleep was fitful and dreams were nightmarish, and years and years of jail time, dull, fatiguing, debilitating, depressing and desolating, stretched ahead, nearly all prisoners wrung self-knowledge out of themselves. They just kept quiet about it (all prisoners observe the code of omertà when it comes to their psyches), and it would be years before I learnt that only by being still could I enable those with whom I worked to derogate from their omertà and let what was inside out, so that they could then turn their hard-won truths into literature. Stillness was everything.

'The Devil walks here' (Friday, 31 May 1996)

First thing Friday morning, the film crew and I left the office in south Belfast and headed for our location on the city's northern side. Once we got to north Belfast proper, a spectacle of urban decline unfolded left and right: decaying Victorian buildings housing businesses (chippers, convenience stores, dog-grooming and tanning salons, funeral undertakers, betting shops); industrial units, squat and ugly, making refrigerators, workwear, wheel trims; cracked pavements where whey-faced people floated, looking disillusioned, exhausted; gutters with drifts of rubbish (cans, beer bottles, Styrofoam containers, KFC boxes); forlorn rubbish patches of scrubby waste ground strewn with pushchairs, bicycles, burnt-out cars, mattress springs, oil drums, microwaves with doors missing, and all showing great circular scorch marks made by the Eleventh Night bonfires; gable ends with monotonous messages ('Fuck the RUC', 'Up the RA', 'Kill all Catholics'); heavily fortified police stations with high paint-splattered walls, impregnable steel gates (always shut) and wild rigs of cameras and communication masts, fortresses constructed to suborn; side streets of red-brick terraces with houses missing, an impression of endless toothless mouths; peace lines zig-zagging in the distance. I wonder, in a hundred years, will everything be gone but these? It all depends on how inclined we are to correct our delinquencies. Currently, it would seem our appetite for self-improvement is small.

We arrived at our location, parked and walked up an entry: high brick walls left and right inset with doors that opened into the back yards of the terraced houses on either side. A few flattened Durex looking like dead fish. Halfway up we reached our goal: one evening, a few months ago, a woman accused of 'anti-social behaviour' was brought here from her house just behind. She was beaten, shorn and doused with green paint, and the paint that had run off her had formed huge pulpy scabs on the walls and roadway. I'm directing a film about punishment beatings and rituals in Northern Ireland (of course, punishment communicates no sense of the barbarism of these events) and, inspired by Eugène Atget's photographs of Paris street scenes, which some critics say are not photographs of Paris 'street scenes' but rather photographs of crime scenes, we'd come to film this crime scene, this splattered stretch of entry, malign and unsettling.

While the shots were being taken, I went around to the street where the victim had lived. In the entry I was in shadow but out on the street I was in the sun, and it was so bright I had to squint. There were shredded Sinn Féin Forum election posters in the gutters (it was the day after the Forum elections). The houses were neat, net curtains in the windows, the sound of children playing. A woman came out of her house. I could see she was watching me. She'd come out to check on me. I went over to her. She was somewhere between forty and sixty, bright-blue, angry eyes and arms folded in a defensive posture. I explained I was with a crew who were filming in the entry behind and what we were filming and why. She shifted to a less defensive posture on hearing this. As I talked, a teenager shuffled out of the house behind her. He had wide hips and narrow shoulders, and his face was covered with thick blond down. He nodded, detached a brace from his upper teeth and pulled it out of his mouth. It was a mix of plastic and steel. The woman, his mother I assumed, began to speak.

'I was born in Artillery Flats,' she said. 'My ma still lives in the flats. I moved down here when I married and it's shite down here, I can tell you. Lookee –' She pointed at a couple of glue-sniffers up the street, their bags opening and closing like pulsing octopuses. 'Hoods,' she said. 'They like to hang around here, and if the husband goes out to speak to them – you know, "Could you go somewhere else, lads?" – know what they say?'

'No.'

'Fuck off!'

A girl appeared, pushing a buggy. Whistling and clapping from the glue-sniffers. 'Hey, Sharon,' they called, 'give us a smile – it can't be that bad!'

'The peelers were out chasing them ones the other night,' the woman said, meaning the glue-sniffers. 'Chased them up and down the street in the pouring rain … the peelers got absolutely soaked, but didn't get them, of course not. Far too quick, them lads.'

A car appeared and honked its horn at Sharon, who fluttered a hand in acknowledgement before disappearing into a house. The glue-sniffers bolted.

'Shinners,' said the woman, meaning the occupants of the car.

I nodded.

'They're what pass for the police round here.'

The car drew level and four hard men inside the car stared out at us. The heat of their stare on the skin was palpable, frightening. Then a touch of the accelerator and the car went on.

'Where would you like to live?' I asked.

'On a mountain,' she said. 'Far, far away.' She gestured at the car that had just passed as it turned at the bottom of the street. 'Those bastards … running round in their big fancy cars and having their foreign holidays, and they never done a day's work in their lives, not a day's work, and them always throwing their weight about like they're our lords and masters – why'd I want to live here with them? So other than Mass on Sundays, I just keep to myself. Don't socialise except for the woman next door.'

This was followed by a brisk summary of the sorts of things that in a sectarian society it is necessary to get straight: her neighbour was a Protestant and frequently had her windows broken by them who didn't like Prods. That wouldn't be her, of course. She adored her neighbour. She and her husband were not bitter, and they had raised their son not to be bitter. And because she wasn't bitter, she couldn't abide the hoods or Sinn Féin or, for that matter, the UVF, who occasionally liked to come down to her street, breaking windows and rioting.

'This place is absolute shite,' she said in conclusion, and turned to her son. 'Put your brace in,' she said.

He forced the tracks over his buckled front teeth.

'It's been nice talking to you,' she said. 'Now don't be putting me on the cameras. And don't forget, put it in your film – the Devil walks here.'

She hustled her son in and closed her front door. I heard the sound of locks turning and bolts sliding home.

At lunchtime we went to City Hall, the seat of local government in Belfast, to film at the announcement of the Forum election results. Men from various political parties were standing about in groups, looking threatening, lethal, the atmosphere like a pub before a fight.

In an upstairs corridor we ambushed Gerry Adams (the Sinn Féin president) and Robert, the presenter, asked him when the republican movement was going to kiss goodbye to the bat (meaning baseball bats, which were and are regularly used in punishment beatings).

Adams fled into a room and left us facing a phalanx of minders. 'Why don't you do something about the beatings?' Robert shouted at them.

'But we're trying,' a woman – one of the few – shouted back.

The same woman found us a few moments later and asked Robert who he was.

'Fyodor Dostoevsky,' he replied.

A few moments later Richard McAuley, Adams' press officer, came over to us. He wanted to know what we were doing.

'It's a documentary about punishment beatings and we're making it with Hugh Lewsley,' I explained. Hugh Lewsley was an SDLP councillor in Lisburn who'd been highly critical of the punishments the IRA had been dishing out and who himself had been savagely beaten, for having the temerity to criticise the IRA, by a group of eight or ten masked men who, amazingly, had nothing to do with the republican movement – at least, so Sinn Féin had said. Obviously, they were public-spirited defenders of the punishment culture, then.

McAuley turned to the Sinn Féin party activists. 'They're doing something with that loser Hugh Lewsley,' he shouted, and all the activists began to laugh, their mirth an amalgam of contempt and threat and disparagement and anger and hatred. I felt anxious. At the same time, I knew I had a film to make. I also knew we should have Sinn Féin in the film. I sidled closer to Richard McAuley to try to fix an appointment.

'We're not impressed with your performance earlier,' he said, meaning us ambushing Adams. 'That was unprofessional.'

It was a marvellous moment, really – the spokesman of the party who were associated, though they denied it, with the IRA impugning a film crew for being unprofessional. If we were going to go there, I had plenty to throw at him but didn't. I was emollience personified, and he agreed I should call him over the weekend and he'd see me Monday.

In the afternoon we went up to the Tyndale estate in Ballysillan. With children gathered round, Robert did a piece to camera concerning a father who was beaten with baseball bats – by loyalists, not republicans.

We finished the first take and a small squinting child, who was one of a crowd who'd gathered to watch, called out, 'Hey, mister, you're wrong. It weren't five bairns your man had, it were four, mister, four.'

★

In the mid-nineties the writer Glenn Patterson noticed that, though Belfast had only the one baseball team ('Which is like having a London Underground line with only one stop,' as he put it; he also said, 'They must like playing with themselves' – an even better joke, I thought), sales of baseball bats were booming. And why was this? Answer: it was the ceasefire. Now hostilities were suspended, the paramilitaries couldn't shoot people any more as a punishment, like they used to. They had to be seen to be on ceasefire. However, the punishments must go on – no self-respecting paramilitary organisation could forego that pleasure. So what to do if you couldn't use a gun? Well, hurls, table legs, pool cues, breeze blocks, spades, pickaxe handles, fence posts, et cetera, et cetera, were all available (and deployed), but frankly none of these had much aesthetic finesse or burnish. Your baseball bat, on the other hand … aha … your baseball bat did look lovely in the mitt, almost as lovely as a pistol. Plus, they were easy to buy, cheap to maintain, and they wiped clean in a tick. Importantly, they were also peeler-proof. If the police stopped you at a checkpoint with a baseball bat in your car boot, when you were en route to administer a punishment beating, you could just say, 'Oh, the baseball bat? Well, I'm just going to the park for a knockabout with me mates,' and the peelers had to wave you on. They couldn't take the bat off you. And although the baseball bat was not as lethal as the gun, and more effort was required when you administered a beating than when you shot some miserable recalcitrant youth in the legs or ankles or elbow, a baseball bat – or the beating effected with the baseball bat, to be precise – nonetheless produced the same effect as a firearm: it reaffirmed paramilitary authority and confirmed the organisation's dominance. The message – and it was always the same message, whether it came out of the barrel of a revolver or the thick end of a baseball bat – was thus: the paramilitary organisation whose members administered the punishment were in charge, not the state. They called the shots, and in their area, it was their way or the highway, no ifs, no buts.

Prompted by his realisation about Belfast's solitary baseball team, Glenn wrote a proposal for a documentary about our paramilitary punishment culture, Baseball in Irish History*, the title being a riff on Irish republican and 1916 Easter Rising leader James Connolly's best-known book,* Labour in Irish History *(1910); the proposal found favour with Channel 4; they commissioned a film, with Glenn producing, Robert Wilson (novelist and writer) scripting and presenting, and myself (another bloody writer) directing.*

Hugh Lewsley, one of our main contributors, lived in Twinbrook, a modern housing estate on the outskirts of the city, and the day before the day described above – which was Thursday, and the day when Northern Ireland's voters went to the polls for the proposed Northern Ireland Forum – the crew and I called to Hugh's house quite early. His home was surrounded by a security fence, and his front garden had clearly been used as a refuse dump: it seemed those who disapproved of him registered their disapproval by lobbing their rubbish over his fence. Hugh Lewsley, when we arrived, was tired and ragged. Sinn Féin party workers had woken him at five o'clock that morning putting posters up outside his house. Did they think he needed reminding there was an election? he wondered. We followed Lewsley to his polling station in West Belfast. We wanted to film him going in to the polling station to vote. As we were about to turn on the camera, we noticed a middle-aged woman approaching the entrance. Would she mind waiting, I asked, just for a tick, so we could film Hugh entering the polling station?

'Him?' said the woman, pointing at Hugh Lewsley. 'I'm not going to wait for that stupid shit! Yous can all fuck off … yous and him both.'

The Past Is Never past but Waits Just Out of Sight If One Can Only See It (Monday, 1 September 1997)

I woke early and drove east – a pearly sky and a sense of autumn looming. Autumn comes early to Ulster. The drive was tedious. I was on autopilot, the radio murmuring, thoughts floating, free-associating …

I pulled in to the car park at Ballysillan Primary School a bit before nine o'clock and went inside. Shiny floors, the smell of polish and paper dust and baked radiator paint and a phone ringing far away and then the school secretary, in the instantly recognisable universal school-secretary voice, speaking carefully. The atmosphere of school: orderly, soothing, muffling, unchanged since my childhood.

In the hallway I found the crew waiting. We were there to make a start on a film about the transfer test (originally known as the eleven-plus), the exam children need to pass to go to grammar school. In England the eleven-plus has largely disappeared, lingering on only in a few counties like Kent and Buckinghamshire, but in Northern Ireland we've kept it. (Oh, how we love to cleave to the old English ways.) The crew and I slipped into the P7 class – they being the cohort who'd be taking the exam – and filmed the children listening to the teacher explain how the coming weeks and months were to be organised.

Those who would sit the test had concentrated expressions as they listened, but something else was also showing – not exactly embarrassment, but something like it: they were getting a kind of attention that the other children weren't and, given their keen sense of natural justice, that didn't sit right with them. They were almost apologetic about the advantages that they might gain. Those who wouldn't be sitting the test, the majority, wore a different look. They knew they were being written off (though this wasn't the school's doing: it was society's). They knew their life chances would be significantly less than those of the children who would go to grammar school if they passed the transfer test because of the advantages grammar schools bestow. Yes, only ten years old but they knew these things. They knew them even if they couldn't have expressed themselves using the words I did. That understanding would only come later, when they were older, by which time it would probably be too late to return to education. If there was any justice in the world, those who are in charge would have been there and studied the faces and seen what there was to see, but they weren't. They never are, because society is organised so that those in charge never have to experience what children think and feel.

After we finished filming, the cameraman, David Barker, and I headed north away from Belfast on the Old Larne Road. At Kilwaughter we got onto the moor that fringes the Glens of Antrim: it was russet coloured, empty, stirring. At Carnalbanagh Sheddings (what a name!) we turned for Glenarm and drove to our destination – Old Church Farm, patrimony of the Morrow family. Ernie, the last Morrow still in residence and a man who still lived like his ancestors, has been proposed as the subject of a documentary film. I am to write the proposal and David will shoot the film.

The way in to the farmhouse was not through the front door but the back door, where I saw the latch had a piece of grubby tin nailed underneath to keep it upright and pert – a classic bit of rural improvisation. And at the sight of this bit of tin, I felt the inner click that comes when something seen in the present catalyses the abrupt shooting up, as if from the seabed, of a past place and the world in which that place is enveloped ... Thus I found myself standing not just at a door at the rear of a farmhouse in County Antrim, but also at the kitchen door of Drewsborough House in east County Clare, with its blue stone steps, up and down which I sprang, day in, day out, during the long summer holidays I spent with my maternal grandparents as a child; and this sense that I was simultaneously in two worlds, which started at this moment, lasted for the duration of the visit.

We went inside and found our way through to the kitchen. Its smell was a mixture of bread, nicotine, stewed tea, house dust, dirt, soap and the glue on the flypaper – a rigid mahogany-coloured curl, studded with what looked like raisins, which hung in a corner – odours I recognised and with which I felt instant kinship, for these were also the odours of the kitchens of the Irish part of my childhood, and they were familiar, comforting.

The kitchen was a dark room, linoleum on the floor, a gas lamp dangling from the ceiling and an old cream-coloured stove. Ernie Morrow was standing at the sink, a grizzled seventy-nine-year-old, in boots tied with yellow laces and absurd tracksuit bottoms. He immediately started speaking, and I could barely understand more than one word in twenty: he speaks pure Ulster Scots. But I could gather, even if the sense eluded me, that his language was extraordinarily vivid and full of powerful turns of phrase and arresting images.

We went with Ernie to the meal house, where the feed for his fowl was stored. He loaded meal into a bucket and its delicious smell was identical to the feed my grandmother fed to her chickens, which was gratifying. We left the meal house and followed Ernie as he traipsed from one outhouse to another, released his birds – ducks, hens and guinea fowl – and fed them. As he went Ernie talked all the time (not even pausing when one of the cats slunk by with a live rat clamped in its mouth, tail waving, feet paddling), and now I'd had a chance to tune in, I began to make sense of what was being said. One story concerned the cunning acquisition of a thresher and a bailer at a knockdown price; a second concerned a will; a third some piece of chicanery that allowed his father to get his old-age pension before he was due it; and a fourth was about the television licence that he is now obliged to buy, since the shop where he got his black-and-white television (powered by generator – there's no mains electricity) passed on his name to the television licensing authorities. Ernie took a very dim view of this betrayal. In his universe, it doesn't do to tout (though this was not the word he used) to the authorities.

We returned to the kitchen and Ernie's talk changed. Now his subjects were his youth, his expertise with horses, his fearlessness, the accidents he survived and the deaths of others (he has an extraordinary memory for names and dates); the point of these stories seemed to be that, in comparison to all these others who had dropped dead in their fifties and sixties, he, Ernie, was still hale and hearty, clearly a physiological miracle. Which brought us, inevitably and neatly, to the revelation (the keystone of the arch of everything he said) *that he had not made a will* – as I would have guessed had he not told me – and nor would he be making a will. Of course not. To make a will was to invite death and Ernie, like so many Irish bachelors, including many I met in my childhood, wasn't prepared to do that.

Two more things that struck me.

One: Ernie knows he has a strong smell (because he doesn't much wash either his clothes or himself), and for this reason he doesn't like to leave Old Church Farm and go to Glenarm or wherever, he explained. Although he lives alone and is a little eccentric, he has not lost his sense of how others see him, and he doesn't want to be known as a person who smells. He has his pride, a countryman's pride – again, something I remember from childhood and admire. The modern tendency of going against agreed social norms is not for him or his ilk.

Two: there is a lavatory but Ernie prefers to use the fields. As we left and started bumping away down the drive, we saw him setting off for the woods with a spade and newspaper. There was another moment from my own childhood.

I thought Ernie Morrow was a good subject for a film. He embodies an old value system (parochial, quietist, rural, hard-working, frugal, even anti-consumerist) that we venerate but have no truck with any longer. Of course, figures like Ernie have been the subject of Irish films in the past. Typically, such subjects live in the west and are Catholic and they embody an idea, and ideal, of Irishness that has its roots in the ideology of the Free State. But Ernie – and this is his USP – lives in the north, is loyal, staunch and Protestant, and so he reminds us that the old value system, when it flourished, was never the property of any single community: it was cross community.

We drove back to Belfast along the coast; the North Channel's waters were gunmetal grey and streaked with white foam. I said little, as I was still half in my past in my grandparents' house in east Clare, the leaving of which (eventually that had to happen, I had to forsake my memories) was as unwelcome as getting out of a warm bed on a cold morning.

★

I made Put to the Test *in Ballysillan, a working-class, largely Protestant (or loyalist, if you prefer) estate in north Belfast. Unemployment was high in Ballysillan. There were many single-parent families. They were many families who survived off benefits. It was a poor place, like many similar estates in England, but unlike the equivalent estates in England, the place had an additional burden: it was rotten with paramilitaries doing their slow, corrosive, destructive work and making a bad situation a whole lot worse. We bumped into paramilitarism and its doleful effects all the time, but the most memorable moment for me came when we were interviewing a mother, Mrs McTaggart, whose shy blond son Magnus was one of the handful of children who did sit the transfer test. One evening, when we were in Mrs McTaggart's house talking, there was a rap at the front door. Mrs McTaggart answered it and then summoned Magnus, whom she sent off with the caller.*

'That poor man,' she said, when she came back. She meant the caller at the door. 'He was beat last year. [She meant by local loyalist paramilitaries; the beating being a punishment beating.] It was a case of mistaken identity, and they beat him so bad he's that way now he can't hardly move, poor fella. He's a cripple. Anyways, he's locked out of his house, he hasn't a key, and with his injuries so bad, he can't even climb in his own window. So I sent Magnus down to climb in and open the door for him. He's a good lad is Magnus.'

NOTICES
GOD so loved
the World, that
He gave His only
begotten Son, that
whosoever believeth
in Him should not
perish, but have
everlasting life
MEETINGS
JESUS
SAVES

On the Day, Averting My Eyes (Friday, 22 May 1998)

I woke early, the bedroom full of light. I went straight to the study to make a few notes about what I had done the previous day, Thursday 21 May, when I was in Maghaberry, where I'd just transferred from the Maze Prison and where I am working as writer-in-residence. I had tracked down a copy of Primo Levi's *If This Is a Man* and *The Truce* for a prisoner in the punishment block (here the cells are smaller than in the normal common-or-garden cells: no television, no radio, no socialising or association, and one hour's solitary exercise in the yard per day); I had gone over a piece about a Dublin pub shooting with a man who was trying to write it up; I had spoken to a prisoner who wanted to write about the RUC's attempt to recruit him as an informer; and I had talked at length to a prisoner who, having just had two days of visits from his wife (she'd seen him in visits, overnighted in a B&B, seen him again in visits the following day), was, in his own words, 'depressed, distressed, vomiting and coming down from the high induced by the visits'. I had also been given a hanky with a picture on it of Timon from *The Lion King* as a thank-you present by a prisoner I was helping with his poetry.

Notes made, I went down to my polling station, the Model Primary School, arriving at about 7 a.m., which was when it opened, for today was the day of the referendum on the Good Friday or Belfast Agreement. Inside the Model there was a smell of Dettol, paper, pencil shavings. I went to the second desk, where people whose initial is 'G' are processed. I showed my polling card and my Irish passport.

'Gébler, Karl Ernest …' was announced by an election official, and another official repeated the name back and scored my name off the roll. I was given my ballot paper. I went to a little booth, a rickety plywood thing with beige curtains, flattened my ballot on the wooden shelf and took the pencil attached to the shelf by a chain.

In the mid-nineties I had gone into HMP Maze (Long Kesh if you prefer) to do creative writing with republican and loyalist prisoners, and during the course of our classes the prisoners (both kinds) talked to me and told me things that I otherwise wouldn't have known. Though nobody was saying so in public, they said, everybody knew (the prisoners, of course, the government, the Northern Ireland Secretary of State, the Northern Ireland Office, 10 Downing Street, the politicians, civil servants, even the prison officers) that the way things had been done had failed and that to go on doing things as they'd been done was pointless. Nobody could win the war, and nobody could afford to lose the war either, so there would have to be a deal which allowed everyone to try something different, without loss of face, and which they would be able to present to their supporters as, if not outright victory, not outright defeat either.

What exactly this new dispensation would be nobody was saying, and certainly not the prisoners, although I did learn one thing: whatever deal was negotiated and eventually secured, there was one non-negotiable principle, and unless this was agreed they weren't agreeing to anything – and their sway was massive. In history, the prisoners in the Maze said, at the end of an armed conflict, once an agreement was struck, the prisoners of war, the POWs, always went home; and in Northern Ireland, the prisoners were adamant, they too, rather than serving out their sentences, would be going home. My informants, I must add, had no interest in my feelings, cautiously expressed, about their early release, or the fact of their early release being a violation of natural justice, or the effect of their early release on victims and relatives. As far as they saw it, they were soldiers and soldiers didn't need to take heed of such matters. But they did take in that I was sceptical and that I found it hard to believe the British state, after decades of anti-paramilitary rhetoric, would let them go, and so they always added a final caveat in our conversations: 'Why do you think you're here helping us to write?' they would say. And then they would answer their own question: 'It's because the Northern Ireland Office know, just like we know, just like everyone knows, there is an understanding coming – a deal – and we will be leaving, and when we get home, we will need skills, including the ability to use language effectively. War doesn't work – it has been shown not to work. Once the deal is done it'll have to be politics, and you're getting us ready for that ... You're getting us ready for the next phase, for the political struggle.' That's what the prisoners would tell me in various ways and with varying degrees of sophistry, swagger and glee.

Thus, looking down at my ballot, I knew exactly what it would mean to put an X in the 'Yes' box – the men in the Maze would walk and those whose lives they'd ruined would, as the saying goes, just have to suck it up. But I knew I couldn't not approve the agreement. If I wanted the north sorted, if I wanted the mess to end, the Belfast or Good Friday Agreement was the only way that could be made to happen. Only voting 'Yes' would get us out of the jam we were in. Nothing else would do that.

Of course, there was another reason to vote 'Yes', which was more persuasive than any political understanding I might have. When we arrived in 1989 we had two children, a daughter and a son; since then, we'd had three more children, a son, a daughter and another son (born in January 1998, only three months before the referendum). We were now agreed, my wife and I, they'd all be schooled in this place. Thus, as far as my heart was concerned, to vote 'Yes' was to vote for a better future for my children, which was a different reason to voting 'Yes' because of what I'd learnt from serving prisoners. And this morning, the political and the personal came together. I made my X in the 'Yes' box. Then I popped my ballot into the box, drove home, made a pot of coffee and went to my desk. I didn't think about what I'd done, as I couldn't grapple with what I knew would happen if the vote went the way I hoped. Yes, my children's lives would hopefully be better, but for all those who'd been hurt by the Troubles (what a disgusting euphemism), it would be a very different story. And how did I manage those feelings? I reverted to the old Gébler default whenever I feel queasy or troubled: I averted my gaze from the facts and buried myself in literature. That's what I did after voting in the historic Northern Irish referendum: I worked on my book (meaning *Father & I*, my memoir) and that way avoided thinking about what would flow from what I'd done.

P · I · R · A

Christmas without Juice (New Year's Day, Friday, 1 January 1999)

I'm writing this on New Year's Day because only today have I been able to catch up, journal-wise, on the Christmas that's just passed.

Christmas Day 1998, Friday a week ago – how strange to note this was last year! – my wife, the five children and I were at home in our house outside Enniskillen, and nothing happened, nothing I remember, but the next day, St Stephen's Day, or Boxing Day, that was different.

Sometime in the afternoon when it wasn't yet dark, though I knew it would very soon become very dark, I stopped in the hall by the barometer, the one I'd inherited from my father. The needle was as low as it could go. Some unpleasant climactic event was coming, no doubt about it. It was in the air. The electric lights wavered and went off, and in the living room the television signal collapsed and the screen went black. Then the lights came back on and the TV fizzed back to life. I decided to get the storm lamps from the shed.

Outside, the sky was the colour of zinc and the wind howled. *This is like walking in a wind tunnel*, I thought as I tramped across the playground towards the shed. I opened the shed door carelessly, and a ferocious gust snapped it back against the lintel and some of the screws holding the hinges popped out and pattered onto the concrete. The world was out of joint, no doubt about it.

I found my lamps, both caked with bird muck, shoved the door shut and fled back inside the house. A few minutes later, I was in the kitchen cleaning the glass of one of the lamps when I heard a rumble unlike anything I'd ever heard before. It was coming from the direction of the electricity pole that supported a grey transformer and that was on the edge of our garden. I looked up and saw a great ball of fire drop from the transformer and slide down the pole like an animal to the ground. All the lights in the house wavered and then they went out, and this time, they did not come back.

The children broke out their torches and chased about the darkening house, squealing with excitement. I went out and got wood and banked the pot-bellied stove. The fire roared and water kettled in the stove's back boiler. Later, when I turned on the kitchen tap, the water was scalding. My wife lit dozens of candles. She set them in every room, on every shelf and ledge and surface. The house looked like a church. There was a lovely smell of warm wax. I lit the lamps as well but they gave off a lamp-oil smell, a fishy smell, not nearly as nice.

There were twelve coming to lunch the next day, Sunday, 27 December. So that Saturday, St Stephen's Day evening, by candlelight, my wife made apple strudel and roasted a ham using the old 1945 New World gas cooker she'd bought in Shepherd's Bush market in London for £5 sometime in the early 1970s. The cooker, because of its age, had holes everywhere, including its back plate, which meant we could see the gas jets roasting the ham reflecting on the kitchen wall behind.

We whiled away the rest of the evening playing pool on a little pool table that one of the children had got for Christmas. It was impossible to distinguish orange from red by candlelight except by lifting the ball from the table and bringing it to the flame. The opportunities for cheating were endless but no one tried. Later we played Jenga and, because we couldn't see, we built a much higher structure than we would have if there had been light.

At the end of the night, the children read aloud to each other from *Harry Potter and the Philosopher's Stone*, published June 1997, another Christmas present.

It took a long time for several hours to pass that miraculous evening. Time went much more slowly without electricity. It was also less fractious. I didn't have to say to the children that, no, they couldn't watch *Men Behaving Badly*. I didn't once have to explain the nine o'clock watershed. I didn't have to ask if the volume could go down on *Jungle Mania 94 (16 Absolutely Firing Jungle Anthems)*. I didn't have to intervene because one child had usurped another's turn on *Crash Bandicoot*. With no power, all the usual points of friction were simply impossible. They simply couldn't happen. At bedtime, I even heard one son mutter, 'I quite enjoyed myself this evening.'

In the morning, I woke to the stove being riddled by my wife and one of the children shouting, 'Oh, it's my dream come true.' I opened my eyes and looked out. It had snowed overnight. And even more miraculously, two burly men from Northern Ireland Electricity appeared on the doorstep ten minutes later.

'We'll fix that transformer now,' one said. I felt unexpectedly depressed by the news. No power might mean more chores, but life without television was quieter, better even.

'You noticed I didn't encourage them,' said my wife when the NIE men left the doorstep and went to their van to get their stuff.

She put kindling in the stove and it caught with a roar.

'We'd better get cracking,' she said. 'The guests will be here at one.'

The children raced out to the snow. Five minutes later, dripping with slush, they were back in, wet and rosy-cheeked. We put their soaking things by the roaring stove. Woollen mittens went bone dry in minutes by this method. Outside, the NIE men laboured at our pole. The power came and went and came and finally went again.

'Good,' said my wife.

But a few minutes later the power was back on, definitively this time.

'Whoopee,' the children cried, rushing in a mob for the television. '*EastEnders*.' They clearly didn't share my adult aversion to power. But my wife did. She now went around the house and turned off every light that had come on and the central heating as well. She wanted our electricity-less life to linger for a while.

The guests came and went. At bedtime, as the children raced down the corridor, they screamed, 'It's cold. We're going to report you for cruelty to children.' Yes, it was cold; we'd kept the heating off in order to extend the illusion of electricitylessness. They got under their covers and didn't show their faces until the next morning.

On Monday, 28 December, there was still snow and I went out in search of sledges. I found some in the stockroom in the toyshop in town: I got two for a tenner. The electricity came and went again all that day too, but we mostly kept it off and we only used it once, briefly, for a spot of hoovering. Yes, otherwise, we went without because it had been so lovely going without. Only at night-time, when no one noticed, did I fire up the central heating just before bed.

'Oh no,' said my wife, when I met her a few moments later, clutching an armful of hot-water bottles she'd prepared and was about to put in everyone's beds. She didn't approve of the central heating being back on. 'There isn't quite that quality of sharp coldness,' she said, 'that makes getting into bed with a hot-water bottle all the nicer, is there, not if the central heating is on?'

It was still pretty cold but I agreed. With the heating on it wasn't as deliciously cold.

'I can hear the boiler rumbling,' she said. 'Oh well, that really is the end of my Christmas,' she added.

Tuesday, 29, Wednesday, 30, Tuesday, 31 December followed, days of snow, tobogganing, snowman-building, slithering, sliding, snowball-making, snowball-throwing and endless drying in front of the pot-bellied stove of wet coats and scarves and mittens and coats and the evocative smell every day of damp wool drying and sometimes wool scorching when it was too hot, and though the electricity was generally back (now and again it did go off but only for a while) there was a lovely shared sense among the family that the best night of the season, the best night of the year, was the candlelit one, when we couldn't tell the colour of the balls on the little pool table.

And now, on the first day of the New Year, and the start of the last year of the twentieth century, already what is so very recent – that short time when the electricity was off – seems historical and lost. The speed with which we hurtle on is dizzying as well as terrifying. Could we just go a little slower occasionally and not rush so much?

The Presentation of the Self: an Evening with Fay Weldon (Friday, 31 March 2000)

In her early working life Fay Weldon was a copywriter. 'Go to work on an egg' is hers, apparently, coined in the 1960s for the Egg Marketing Board's campaign to get people eating more eggs. The slogan, still remembered, indicates she is a person with a certain kind of intelligence and the ability to make things with language that stick to the psyche like burrs stick to clothing. This is something I can't do.

From copywriting, Fay Weldon moved to literature. She wrote a number of highly addictive novels, three of which have been adapted for television: *The Life and Loves of a She-Devil* (BBC2, 1986), *The Cloning of Joanna May* (ITV, 1992) and *Big Women* (Channel 4, 1998). I'm interviewing Fay Weldon in Belfast and I've watched them all, and read several Weldon novels besides, and my principal thought at the end of my Weldon binge is that she has no truck with plausibility or accuracy or psychological verisimilitude: her people are impossible, unlikely, far-fetched, improbable, and her plots are exaggerated and even cartoonish, yet her fans and the television commissioning editors who keep dramatising her novels aren't in the least bit bothered because to their minds her work speaks a truth, or even *the* truth, about the miseries of modern sexual politics. It also helps that, with the exception of the joke-free novel *Praxis* (which some regard as her best) and *Puffball* (which in my opinion is her best), none of the work ever really hurts you. You're never going to cry after a Weldon. She's no Kafka taking the axe to your frozen heart.

When one closes a Weldon book or finishes watching a Weldon on telly, one is discombobulated, but the discombobulation is followed by the comforting thought, *Well, that was different! Food for thought there*, and the knowledge that at the next dinner party one attends, with other like-minded members of the bourgeoisie, one will be able to have a conversation about the Weldon with the other guests as one tucks in, vis-à-vis her relevance to culture and modern relationships. And a jolly good conversation it will be (challenging, progressive, topical, radical) because – and I don't say this cynically – her art is absolutely perfect for the culture; for everything we need to discuss, at least when it comes to men and women, her work is the gateway.

Today was the day of the event. I arrived at the venue in Belfast about 5.30 p.m. and went in search of Miranda, the organiser. We'd never met, all our dealings having been by letter.

I found Miranda in her office. Something about the shape of her face and the way that she sat reminded me of Louise Brooks, and yet she didn't have the bob.

'You live in Derryhillagh School?' she said.

'I do.'

She knew it, she said. Knew it well. Very well. A relative had been headmistress of Derryhillagh. And Miranda had stayed with her in Enniskillen and had often been taken to the school when she was on holiday, and while her relative did headmistressy things, she'd played. She therefore knew the schoolhouse, now my house, with its two square classrooms and high ceilings and long back corridor with the shiny polished concrete floor, and its boys' entrance and its girls' entrance and its cloakrooms with the huge hooks (which our own coats now hang from) and its humpy garden patch where the pupils were taught to grow vegetables and its bottleneck well with its beautiful brick walls and its stream lined with alders and rowan trees and its lovely metal front gates to one of which was attached the letterbox. I told her the box had now been colonised by little birds, tits I thought, who had made nests of sheep's fur at the bottom and darted in and out through the letter slot. In her day, she explained, this wouldn't have happened, as there were letters coming daily, but she did like the idea of the little birds living now inside it.

I would have liked to have asked Miranda more about her childhood visits and what the schoolhouse was like in those days when it was still a working school (it was decommissioned in 1973) but I couldn't because there was Fay Weldon. She was smaller than I'd expected and very compact. She was smiling heavily and her face was lined with the lines which come from smiling heavily all the time. She looked Russian – or would have if she'd been bundled in a big coat and fur-lined boots. Her voice was low, quiet, and her accent had just a trace of New Zealand, the place where she was reared. She seemed shy, even reticent – at least, that was my first impression.

We were all booked to eat together before the interview. We toddled off to the restaurant, sat down, and within seconds my putative interviewee was talking about therapists. (So much for my first impression – shyness! reticence! – I couldn't have been more wrong.) She and her husband, Ron Weldon, a jazz musician and antiques dealer, had both visited therapists regularly during their marriage; the therapy was meant to improve things only it didn't because, as she explained, Ron became entangled with his therapist.

'So, I rang this therapist,' she continued (oh, here was a line to make me sit up), 'and I said, "He doesn't talk to me because he talks to you so much." And do you know what she said?'

There was a pause.

'"Keep it like that, because if he was to start with you, he'd never stop talking, ever."'

Persuaded by this therapist that his and his wife's astrological signs were incompatible – this was according to Fay, but I believed her – Ron left Fay for … well, the therapist with whom, presumably, he was astrologically compatible. Divorce proceedings were initiated, but hours before they came through, Ron died, so technically he and Fay were never divorced. She was still Mrs Weldon. This story had a depth of hurt that wasn't in her written work, and I wondered why she hadn't written more in this register. I would have liked books with this kind of pain much more than the books she published. Naturally, I didn't vocalise my thoughts.

From therapy, we moved to guilt. Where else was there to go?

'I believe in guilt,' said Fay.

Miranda looked appalled. Was she hearing right? Fay Weldon, the radical, feminist, mischief-making contrarian, had she actually said, 'I believe in guilt'?

Oh, indeed she had, for she continued: 'Guilt is the moral equivalent of pain. You feel guilty until you either stop doing what you're doing because you *are not* meant to, or you do what you're not doing because you *are* meant to. But either way, the guilt won't go away *until you act*. That's what guilt does: it makes you do right and it's marvellous, absolutely marvellous, really, it is.'

'But guilt is bad, surely,' said Miranda reasonably.

'No. It's good.'

Next Fay began to interrogate Miranda about her life; Miranda surely had something she should feel guilty about and Fay was determined to unearth this. But every question drew a blank. Nothing in Miranda's life, it seemed, was a reason for guilt.

'Don't you have an old mother to go and see?' said Fay finally, sounding as if this really wasn't the card she wanted to play. She definitely wanted a better occasion for guilt than the old-mother card.

'Both my parents are dead,' said Miranda.

But Fay wasn't going to be deterred. She was going to find something Miranda could feel guilty about.

'Don't you have anyone you have to be responsible for at Christmas?' she said.

'No,' said Miranda. 'I just do what I want. I spend it by myself or I ask my brother over.'

Fay changed tack. 'We're not meant to live alone,' she said. 'We're meant to live with other people and we're meant to take responsibility for them.'

Ah, if she couldn't get Miranda on guilt she'd get her on this, I thought.

'Get married and have some babies. Twins, I think, in your case,' Fay continued. 'You need some duty and the guilt will help you to keep going.'

I sat there thinking, *This does not compute*. I could see Miranda thinking the same. Then she spoke. Why, she asked, was Fay telling her that to be a woman with no attachments and endless choices was *not* right? Surely the reverse was true? For most of history women were beset by duty and had been made to feel guilty about not doing their duty. Wasn't it a good thing to not be entangled by those old norms? I noticed she was speaking generally and not about herself. *That was astute*, I thought. A good way to de-escalate.

Fay heard Miranda out and then just repeated her counsel: Miranda should marry, have babies. She needed to be responsible. She needed to be engaged. She needed to suffer pain. It crossed my mind that envy was in play. Hence the tirade. Miranda was leading a life Fay had never had and she resented this. Could that be it? Or was this just what Fay thought? That seemed more likely. But also oh-so improbable. I didn't know and I wasn't up to finding out, either. In her pomp, Fay was formidable. I didn't want to probe; I didn't want to take her on. Nor did Miranda. So she didn't push back, she just let it go, her future and how she should live, and we moved on to the Booker Prize and the state of British television.

After dinner, we went across to the venue to do the event, and the astonishing but interesting moral contrarianism that Fay had offered up over dinner about the importance of moral pain in the life of the suffering human being vanished, and instead Fay only said the things she had already said in public a thousand times about men and the patriarchy and husbands and love, blah, blah, blah. The audience were there to see her play the Fay they knew, and they were happy, but her performance wasn't a patch on the one I'd witnessed over dinner. Give me Old Testament Fay, hard, adamantine, rigorous and judgemental, over modern Fay any day.

The best part of the interview was where Weldon laid out her taxonomy of literature, which, though I felt sure she'd repeated it many times before, was still worth hearing. It also showed the copywriting intelligence was still firing.

'There are four categories,' she began. 'One, there are good-good books. That's the classics. You read these books because you have to but you don't necessarily enjoy them. Then there are the good-bad books. These are the books – thrillers, for instance – that you enjoy but which you know aren't great literature as you read them.'

Here she went into a long peroration about the joy of buying thrillers in Heathrow to read on the plane; I had a vague idea the good-bad book was an idea from somewhere else. Orwell? I wasn't sure.

'Then there are the bad-good books. Those are the books written by authors with grants from the Arts Council. And then there are the bad-bad books. They're the awful, trashy books, which are just unreadable rubbish.'

Though I pushed her, she wouldn't name any books in any category. She was too fly to fall into a trap like that.

I drove home listening to Arundhati Roy's Booker Prize-winning *The God of Small Things*, the melancholy story of fraternal twins whose lives are destroyed by the Love Laws prevalent in 1960s Kerala. After a bit, I turned the tape off and began to wonder, having heard Weldon's taxonomy, how to classify what I'd been hearing: a good-good book? No, that wasn't right. Whatever else it did, *The God of Small Things* gave pleasure, which the good-good book apparently didn't. Was it a good-bad book, then? No. That wasn't right, either. It was literature, it was literary. So Fay's system hadn't worked with the very first book I'd attempted to categorise. But then I saw my mistake. In my wrong-headed way, I'd taken her literally. Fay's taxonomy wasn't actually a system for categorisation. It was a schtick to get people sparring, sparking, fizzing, which of course, as I drove, was precisely what it had done for me.

In the literary Anglosphere we have a perverse attitude to difficulty and ease. Novels categorised as 'no fun and requiring a lot of effort to read' are regularly compared unfavourably to those we hold to be 'great fun and requiring little or no effort to read'. The latter are held to be anti-elitist and democratic. Weldon's four-categories conceit is underpinned by a preference for easy over hard. But why, because a book is easy, is it better? Surely all it is is easier. And why can't we accept that sometimes good things are hard? Or is our preference for easy over hard a sign that we just want our literature to be like everything else we consume – customer-friendly, relatable and the rest? But speeding westwards in my darkened metal box, following the curve of the motorway, eyes on the red tail lights of the vehicle ahead, answer came there none.

★

In 2000, Fay Weldon (1931–2023) became a member of the Church of England and was confirmed at St Paul's Cathedral. Over dinner, I like to think, I'd had a signal of what was coming, though I wasn't to know that till later.

Where I Was (Tuesday, 11 September 2001)

At about five thirty an officer from the prison rang.

'Have you seen the news, mate?' he'd asked. He had an Antrim twang, very charming.

No, I said. I was in my study, which is in an old bicycle shed separate from the house, and I'd been there since nine in the morning working on a history of the siege of Derry I'm writing. I had no television. I hadn't had the radio on either. So, no, I hadn't seen the news.

'Flipping planes smashing into the Twin Towers in New York,' he explained. 'It's surreal.'

Another friend had telephoned and told him, he continued, and so now he was phoning to tell me. It's what Good Samaritans do, he said. They pass on the news, don't they?

A few minutes later my second son, fresh from school, burst into my study.

'Dad,' he said, 'there's planes crashing into New York.'

I went into the schoolhouse and turned on the television and watched the special news bulletin about the attacks in New York, Washington and Pittsburgh. And as I watched, I split internally. One part of me was in the moment, watching and reacting; this part was in the grip of confusion and fear, dismay and disbelief. What I was seeing, I felt, had an unreality about it. *It can't be true*, I thought, although I also knew it was. The other part of me was set back from the me that was reeling; this part was watching the part that was watching and reacting to the television. This part was observant, cool, gnomic, prescient and it offered this prediction: what I was seeing would be the first event, since President Kennedy's assassination, about which almost everyone in the Western world would later be able to say that they knew exactly where they were and what they were doing when they saw it.

Seán MacBride (Friday, 28 June 2002)

The board of the Arts Council typically meet in Dublin but we like to show our faces in the country now and again, and so to Markree Castle, a country hotel in County Sligo, we went. We had our meeting and then the board had dinner together in the dining room and I was sat opposite Proinsias Mac Aonghusa, also a board member. I like him: he is loquacious, genial and surprising. His favourite author is Graham Greene. We have often talked about Greene, a great writer, we agree, despite his tin ear, whose dialogue, though always efficient, is never exhilarating. He's no Harold Pinter.

As we were chatting, waiting to give our orders, I noticed that Proinsias saw something or someone and it made him smile. He was pleased about something.

'See him.' Proinsias pointed at a man in a cravat taking orders at another table.

'Yes,' I said, as I watched this figure scribble something then glide on to the next diner. He was medium height, medium build and had a very straight back.

That man, Proinsias explained, was Charles Cooper, the current owner of Markree Castle and the grandson of Major Bryan Cooper, a unionist who'd sat in Dáil Éireann. The major, he continued, was also the one who alibied Seán MacBride after he was charged with Kevin O'Higgins' murder.

'We've talked about MacBride before,' said Proinsias – we had: he was another topic of conversation, along with Greene – 'so you'll like this.'

Yes, I thought, *I will* …

In the early 1970s Seán MacBride was an occasional visitor to my mother's house in Chelsea, London. I would have been fifteen, sixteen, seventeen years old. At this point in his life, MacBride was a senior Irish statesman. He'd been in government in Ireland and now he was going global. He was the founder of Justice, which later became the UK section of the International Commission of Jurists. He was active in a number of international organisations concerned with human rights, among them the Prisoners of Conscience Appeal Fund. He was the chair of Amnesty International. Other glories and honours were pending: his Nobel Peace Prize (1974), his Lenin Peace Prize (1975–6) and his UNESCO Silver Medal for Service (1980). At the time I wasn't across the detail, but I got the drift: he was a big deal.

In person he was a dandy. He wore beautiful clothes (including, sometimes, a waistcoat – a bad move, I'd decided: only John Bull and imbeciles from the Monday Club wore waistcoats). He spoke in a funny accent – it was both French and not French at the same time – and when he did he had a way of holding his head back and looking down his nose at you. It wasn't a haughty thing. It wasn't disdainful. It was just not normal. *Why can't he just hold his head straight and talk like a normal person?* I always thought when he was gabbing away. And he also had this annoying way of leaning on his elbow and supporting his head with his hand, as if his brains were super heavy and needed support. I assumed he thought this pose reinforced his status as an intellectual, but I saw right through it. Such were an adolescent's judgements.

When MacBride came it was usually to lunch, which was eaten in the kitchen, on the first floor. The kitchen was a square room with a single large casement window with a blind that was always half down and on which were painted leaves, branches, blossoms, birds. I think it was Philip Sutton's work. It was colourful, bright, very Henri Rousseau.

In the garden, just outside, there was a huge elm. In summer, when the light shone through the tree's canopy, its leaves stained the light green, and inside the kitchen, with the decorated blind's sylvan scene looming over you, you had the impression it wasn't so much a house in Chelsea where you were sitting but a cool green wood.

For lunch my mother would often serve gazpacho – thin, sharp, cleansing – and smoked salmon on thinly sliced, beautifully buttered brown bread and very dry, crisp white wine; and as we nibbled and sipped, MacBride would talk about himself, his deeds, his insights, his feints, his contrivances and his magnificent subterfuges, all of which inevitably ended in triumph for him and defeat for whomever was agin him. In my eyes, he was a pub bore, one of those opinionated, windy, ghastly types who expected to be listened to reverently and applauded rapturously. I never lingered once I'd eaten.

One of MacBride's self-aggrandising stories, which he told more than once and spun to interminable length when he did, concerned his mother, Maud Gonne, and himself. They were in London. On account of Maud Gonne's Irish republican sympathies, they had a Metropolitan Police tail; they wished to lose this tail, which they did by entering the Jermyn Street Turkish Baths by one door, the copper dutifully following, and then craftily slipping out by a back door which the luckless Mr Plod didn't know about. MacBride appeared to believe this adventure proved that the English (or at least the English police) were stupid whereas the Irish (or at least Irish patriots) were clever. That was his takeaway, when he riffed on it afterwards. I wasn't impressed. The ploy of going in by one door and leaving by another struck me as a childish ruse which wouldn't be out of place in a Tintin book, and I couldn't understand why this man, who supposedly was so very clever, couldn't see that. Perhaps the story suggested he was actually a bit dim – or so I wondered privately. Oh, the harsh judgement of youth.

In 1927, Proinsias began, when MacBride was in the IRA (these were the days when he was a committed armed-force republican, which were long before he became an international statesman), the decision was 'apparently' made to assassinate Kevin O'Higgins, the Free State minister for justice, because of his responsibility for the executions of republicans in the Civil War.

So … it was a Sunday morning, and three anti-Treaty IRA scouts – O'Higgins being away at a conference in Europe – went to recce O'Higgins' home in Booterstown, and sitting in their car, who do they see only O'Higgins, returned early from Europe (the conference had collapsed), walking to Mass.

The plan had been to shoot O'Higgins at a later date, but seeing as chance had afforded this opportunity, the trio opted to do it now. They killed him and fled.

At the time of the assassination MacBride was out of Ireland. The Irish state believed (or found it convenient to believe) MacBride must be involved in the whole filthy business. As soon as he was back on Irish soil, he was arrested and charged with O'Higgins' murder. Come the trial, however, MacBride's defence team produced Major Bryan Cooper, who testified that at the time of Kevin O'Higgins' murder, both he and MacBride had been together aboard a ferry travelling from Britain to Ireland. The major's testimony swung it and MacBride beat the rap. But this triumph couldn't keep him out of jail. The state immediately judged him a subversive and interned him in Mountjoy Prison.

'Anyhow,' continued Proinsias, 'years later, years and years later, I discovered who the ones who killed O'Higgins were and how it happened, and I wrote the story up. Before it was published, I saw MacBride. I said, "I've written this article about O'Higgins' murderers. I felt I should." MacBride said, "Oh no, you mustn't publish, Proinsias." I said, "The men in question are dead." He said, "That doesn't matter. You mustn't publish. There'll be grave repercussions."'

Proinsias continued: 'I said to MacBride, "It's written and it's going into the public domain." And it did, and it was one of my greatest successes. I did very well out of it. And of course, there were no grave repercussions, not for MacBride. After all, time had passed.'

Proinsias smiled. It was a rich, expressive smile. What MacBride meant by 'grave repercussions', the smile told me, was the damage that might arise from the article to himself.

'Very lucky man, MacBride,' said Proinsias. 'Very lucky man.'

We fell silent and stared at Charles Cooper as he filled the wine glasses of the guests at the table where he'd just taken orders. There was so much to like about this moment. There was the collision of past and present, a controversial murder and the sighting of the descendant of a figure of some importance in the original event.

Then there was the story's Greenean feel: Cooper was a unionist who'd been a Westminster MP for a bit, while MacBride was a republican, yet the first had alibied the second, no matter their political differences. That could easily be in a Graham Greene novel.

And finally, there was the connection between what I'd heard and my own past. Perhaps, I thought, remembering the lunches in Chelsea, MacBride's endless boasting about how he always came out on top (oh goodness, he was a windbag) was actually just part of a carefully cultivated persona that he'd created to deflect attention away from what he had actually been in the past, which was a man involved in Ireland's physical-force tradition, a man who had done things which he definitely would not want remembered once he entered his international-statesman phase. MacBride's mannerisms, in other words, were intended to misdirect. Maybe.

Charles Cooper approached with his notebook and pen in hand. 'Can I take your orders?' I heard. I looked at his mild, open face. Was it possible, I wondered, if his grandfather hadn't done what he did, MacBride might have been found guilty and hanged and then I'd never have had lunch with the Irish statesman in the kitchen filled with stained green light?

★

I am a pattern-loving creature and stories, because they're patterned, are a comfort. Facts, on the other hand, are truculent and invariably refuse to form themselves into a comforting pattern. What MacBride's exact position was in the IRA in 1927 is moot. Whether or not MacBride had any clout in the IRA in 1927, enough clout to get a murder going, is moot. Whether or not MacBride ordered the killing of O'Higgins is moot. Whether or not the IRA would have sanctioned the killing of O'Higgins, initiated by MacBride or any other member of the organisation, is moot. Whether or not it was Cooper's alibi that swung it for MacBride with the court is moot. Whether or not the state would have hanged MacBride had the prosecution secured a conviction is moot. But whether or not the story I heard in Markree Castle is now spoiled in the light of these facts is also moot. I think I prefer to leave it alone and unimpugned, so it can do its magical work.

On the Radio (Sunday, 8 June 2003)

I am in the little BBC studio in Enniskillen early on Sunday morning. The main road outside is quiet, nothing stirring, though I can hear bells pealing, the bells of one of the churches at the other end of the town summoning their congregation to worship – oh, the bells of an Enniskillen Sunday, the somnolence of an Enniskillen Sunday …

I am here to participate in a live four-way discussion for *Sunday Sequence* (a BBC Radio Ulster ethics and religious affairs programme) on the autobiography of the loyalist Michael Stone.

On the table in front of me is the note I have prepared on the text, and as I wait, I read and reread it:

> Michael Stone's *None Shall Divide Us*, for the most part, is a disturbing account of either hurting or killing people, as this is largely what the writer has devoted his life to doing. This writer is not interested in persuading us to like him. He simply wants us to know what he did, how he killed this man and whacked that one. He isn't much interested either in the origins or well-springs of his actions or his politics. Republican writers (notably Danny Morrison and Gerry Adams) invariably go to great trouble to demonstrate that they are the product of centuries of unhappiness; not so M. Stone: he is just a soldier who is entirely reactive and who did what he did in response to

IRA malfeasance and violence. It's that simple. Of course, Ulster loyalists are defending a state which was artificially created in order to ensure the advantage of their confession, so it's entirely inevitable they don't have the same melancholy backstories that republicans, who are the descendants of the dispossessed and the oppressed, have. From this it follows that a loyalist's self-image (any loyalist's self-image) isn't that he's a righter of ancient wrongs (that's very much owned by republicans), but rather that he's just a simple soldier loyal to a noble cause (the Union, the Crown). That's nonsense, of course, but the absence of special pleading by Stone is refreshing.

As for the impact of the book, well, it's obviously going to be problematic: it's undoubtedly going to hurt and outrage the relatives of those the writer murdered. Can Stone be stopped? Not as the law currently stands. Should he be stopped? Well, I would answer that question with this question: does his book serve the public interest? Answer: yes, in one sense it does; it's a corrective to the inanity of most popular journalism, which is delighted to demonise our 'enemies' (including loyalists) but makes very little or no effort to understand and explain. Vilification may offer relief, and engagement is always going to be painful and troubling, but the latter has to be better than the former, surely? Unless we engage with the world as it actually is (rather than as we wish it were), how can we ever develop or grow? Stone's book tells us a lot about loyalism, or his brand at any rate, and its reactive, barren, obdurate, unforgiving, bitter pith. Better to know about it than not, I say. From which it follows that I believe it is in the public interest that we read this book and we can only read this book if it is published; so, it should be published. I say this because the paramilitary memoirs

> written by Irish republicans about the War of Independence have also been incredibly useful and educational – at least to me. I learnt a lot about what you need to be if you're going to kill, and the consequences for your psyche of making yourself someone who kills, from Dan Breen's *My Fight for Irish Freedom* and Ernie O'Malley's *On Another Man's Wound*, both of which contain graphic accounts of the killing of RIC policemen and British soldiers. And interestingly, O'Malley's book in its day caused the same sort of furore as Stone's book is causing now. The widows of the three British army officers captured near Fethard in June 1921, whose execution O'Malley ordered and witnessed, strongly objected to his profiting from the book that contained his account (unflinching, pitiless, terrifying) of the execution of their husbands. So, Ernie O'Malley in the last century and Stone in this century – everything's just a repeat, really, or at least in Ireland, so it seems.

I hook up to Belfast and the producer comes on and then off we go, we're live. The other panellists are Dawn Purvis from the Progressive Unionist Party, Duncan Shipley-Dalton, an Ulster Unionist MLA, and Mark Thompson, the organiser of the West Belfast organisation Relatives for Justice. The discussion that follows is utterly predictable. Mr Thompson thinks Stone's book is beyond the pale. It's going to upset the relatives, he says. Fair enough. So therefore what's needed, he continues, is a public inquiry that will examine the whole matter of collusion between Michael Stone and the British security forces. His spiel sounds like an editorial from *An Phoblacht/Republican News* (I'm a regular reader, so I know of what I speak), and though loyalism and the British state are very mixed up, I know, we are here surely to talk about a book as a book and the man who wrote that book, rather than all the bad things wot the Brits have done.

There is also the tiny little matter of how the demand for an inquiry (with its implicit rebuke to perfidious Albion) is going to play with the PUP and the UU representatives who are participating in this discussion. Badly, of course. They don't like what they hear and very quickly our 'discussion' becomes a bad-tempered reiteration of our ancient conflict, a green and orange ding-dong. (Oh yes, we're world famous here for our capacity to pick at the old scab no matter what the subject under discussion is.)

I try to talk literature by blabbing for Ireland about the paramilitary memoir (the genre, and it is a thing) and its place in the culture, but this just makes Mr Thompson even angrier. How dare I talk about culture and Stone. In the end, he has to be asked to stop by the interviewer, but the poison is out and it's all rancour from here on in. An hour later I leave the studio exhausted and feeling poisoned. What on earth was I thinking when I agreed to participate? It was always going to be horrible.

Two Bonuses (Wednesday, 18 August 2004)

Back in June, I wrote this early one morning without really thinking.

'The Line in the Grass'

We speed along the lane on bicycles,
My second son and I, under the trees
Where the crows caw from their twiggy nest balls,
Then zoom up the long strait past Bruce's yard.

The air smells of honeysuckle and manure,
Silage, molasses and tractor exhaust.
It is a bright still summer's evening:
A clear sky and a riot of birdsong.

On the rough patch, outside our parish church,
Eddie, a neighbour, sits in his apple-
Green Astra, reading this week's *Impartial.*
In the churchyard behind, old graves, brown flowers.

We pass the equestrian riding ground,
A square of dirty sand with painted jumps,

Carlo Gébler

Arrive at Leonard's Filling Station and shop
And buy a packet of Werther's toffees.

On the way home on the balcony road
A lolling collie panting in the heat
And a distant view of lower lough Erne
Motionless, like a sheet of beaten tin.

From the top of Macaulay's hill, we see
The schoolhouse below us, laid out in plan:
The sagging privet, my old Vauxhall, the
Bangor blues, shining miraculously.

Pedantically, I say, 'Beware the hill.
It's one-in-ten.' 'No, Dad, I'll cut across
Bruce's field,' he says. 'It's more direct. You
Take the road and we'll see who gets home first.'

I wait while he heaves his bike over the
Rusty top gate tied shut with frayed bailer
Twine, and sets his wheels down in the field where
Knee-length grass sways as if under water.

Then off we race, he his way, and I mine,
And as I drop down the one-in-ten, brakes
Juddering, I keep glancing sideways at
The demon boy, his white shirt billowing,

Hurtling towards the field's bottom gate. When
We meet there, a Werther's clacking against

A Cold Eye

His teeth, he says, 'See, Dad, it's quicker to
Take the field than the long way around by road.'

Later that evening, out at the car, I
Glance sideways, indifferently, casually,
Through my own gate, up the slope of the field,
Which my son had earlier spurted down.

The grass is the blue of a deep still sea
And running down the middle, connecting
Top to bottom gate, is the line he cut,
Like the wake left after a ship's passage.

While swifts dart above me in the air
Making the special soughing sound they make
As they careen and zig-zag, I stand a
Long time and stare at the line in the grass.

Later in the night Bruce's mower, its
Headlamps blazing, harrumphs into the field
To cut, and, come dawn, every blade is chopped,
And waiting for wrapping. The line is gone.

First there is the event, and then there is
What follows after, which is the proof of
Life, the proof of joy: drink in, drink deep, it
Does not last, it does not last, it does not …

I printed this out when it was finished and kept it on my desk for a while. It had come easy, and I hoped its being in view would precipitate something else coming easy. It didn't, so I put it away in my filing cabinet. And there it stayed until I came back yesterday from dropping my oldest son to the airport. I got it out and reread it and overnight it did its work and catalysed something; I'm assuming this anyhow because when I got into my study this morning this came, and like its predecessor, it just wrote itself. If only everything I write could come like this.

'The Football'

As he mows my grass he finds a soggy
Old football: the lace is half-undone. The
White paint that covered it once is flaking
off. When he's finished he boots it with all

The energy of his seventeen years.
It flies through the air and lands heavily
And rolls a bit on the newly cut lawn
Gathering grass blades to its pulpy form,

Then, finally, comes to rest. The next day
I take him to the airport. We part
At Departures through which I've so often
Shepherded him on holidays

But where today I do not. This is his
First solo holiday, first step along
The path, that leads away from parents
To independence. So today I stand

A Cold Eye

With others who have come to say goodbye
And watch my boy with his rolled-up copy
Of *Nuts*, show security his passport
And disappear into the world beyond.

When I get home and get out of the car
My eye flies straight to the football and I
Feel a fierce tightening and gush of loss.
I feel I've been burnt but on the inside.

I want him back, I think, but as I say
The words I not only know they're pointless
But worse, I know that behind them lurks the
Undefeatable fact; we live in time

And that means loss is inescapable.
Who would have thought that a puffy old
Football, could represent the fact that at
The heart of it all lies impermanence.

Dinner with the Booths (Friday, 28 October 2005)

Tony Booth, the star of *Till Death Us Do Part*, the British sitcom, which I watched religiously as an adolescent, came to dinner at the schoolhouse along with his wife. He was a garrulous raconteur and told endless stories about the 1960s when he was simultaneously a huge TV star and – at least according to his own account – a Labour Party activist who energetically worked to advance the cause of socialism in England. All his stories about this period and his left-wing activities were ribald.

For example: 'Can the Labour Party rely on your vote, then?' he asks a white woman who is in bed with a West Indian man in a Notting Hill flat. 'Don't be fucking mad,' she says, 'a vote for you is a vote for the fucking blacks. I vote for you and my street will be full of the fuckers.'

As I listened to our guest trot out one saucy anecdote after another I felt my spirits sinking. It was partly that the great actor I remembered had degenerated into the old campaigner who told preposterous tales of long ago wars, but it was also that all his talk made me remember that in the 1960s I too believed in socialism and the Labour Party (in a naive and ignorant way, of course – it was emotional not rational) and I too believed everything was going to come good and Labour was going to supplant the Tories as the party of government.

And now, here I was – no, here I am, decades on – and it hasn't happened, what either of us had believed or hoped for. And what's more, it isn't going to happen either. The Man has won, at least in the

UK. The market is king. And foreign wars – the invasion of Iraq proves this – are once again a thing. The Tories are currently out of power and therefore unable to ruin people's lives as they like to do (that is what I believe they will always do) but they'll be back and they'll be worse than what we have, and in today's world that's the distinction. It isn't that Labour today are better than the Tories; they are just less bad (and that's why I'd always rather have them in power than the Tories).

Booth, I suspect, finds what's come to pass (Labour's shift from socialism to social democracy, MOR politics and the acceptance of market values) intolerable, and his coping strategy is to tell the tall tales he tells. They cheer him up, I'm sure. I'm not persuaded by this approach, but who's to say if I were in his position, father of the prime minister's wife Cherie Blair and all that, I wouldn't do just the same and spend my time telling tales of long ago and losing myself in lost glories.

★

In Till Death Us Do Part (1966–75) *Tony Booth played Mike Rawlins who is married to Rita (Una Stubbs) who is the daughter of Alf Garnett (Warren Mitchell) and Else (Dandy Nichols). Each episode follows the same schtick: Alf, the father-in-law, a bald white working-class bigot, says appalling things, often about women or immigrants, and his smiling son-in-law, a Scouser with the gift of the gab, aided and abetted by his put-upon mother-in-law and his appalled wife, responds in a logical, lawyer-like way with question following question until Alf, knowing he is outmanoeuvred, eventually explodes in frustrated, splenetic rage.*

I loved the programme. The domestic battles it presented were perfectly timed, dazzlingly executed and very funny. They were also raw and painful: there was nothing else on British television that felt quite so dangerous, or true. Men like Garnett were everywhere then, and it was great to see a programme which showed a bigot and a progressive (or progressives – for it was really Alf versus the other three) locking horns and the progressives winning because they had the better arguments.

Till Death Us Do Part *was controversial. Many thought it wrong to have a character like Garnett airing in public the views he aired. They thought it was unseemly, even if it was true that men like Garnett and the views he articulated were ubiquitous. Scrub the series, they said. Johnny Speight, the deviser and writer of* Till Death Us Do Part, *obviously took the opposite position. He thought the series, featuring and indeed foregrounding a character like Alf, was good for the nation precisely because it showed the British, or the English anyway, a side of the national character they didn't like to admit existed – the jingoist, intolerant, women-hating, fascist side. Speight believed it might or even would do the monsters good to see themselves as they were. At least that was his argument.*

In my experience, however, the series wasn't the corrective it was supposed it might have been; on the contrary, it seemed to have a reinforcing effect, for on buses and tubes, in the cafés and in the street, and at Holland Park Comprehensive where I was a pupil, I would regularly overhear skinheads – for they were everywhere, there was a bloody epidemic of them then – channelling Alf's reactionary attitudes. Oh, how they loved him, even to the extent of sometimes parroting Alf's lines of dialogue lifted straight from an episode the day after it had aired. I did understand, however, in the way an adolescent understands these things that Speight intended good even if those he was minded to goad into better ways weren't minded to change and, on the contrary, perversely drew succour from his critique. This understanding was an important early lesson on what art could and could not do.

I was a thirteen-year-old teenager on 20 April 1968 when the Conservative politician Enoch Powell (much admired by Alf Garnett, of course) delivered his notorious 'Rivers of Blood' speech in which he criticised mass Commonwealth immigration to the United Kingdom. I was only coming into consciousness, but the speech did register. At school I had seen a skinhead break a milk bottle and stick the jagged butt into the face of the milk monitor, who was of Pakistani heritage, while his friends, as the monitor's blood gushed, shouted at their victim that he should fuck off back to where he came from. Actually, West London was where he came from – the monitor's parents had a restaurant and he had an estuarine accent, as I knew on account of his having supervised the milk queue with grace and tact for months. He was an authority figure I very much liked.

I also had several interactions of my own with skinheads. I was variously put through swing doors, thrown down stairs and punched for no reason. One afternoon, when I was on my way home from school and I was on the Putney railway footbridge which spans the Thames, I was accosted by two skinheads several years older than me. They demanded money and when I wouldn't give them any (I had none) tried to throw me off the footbridge. The Thames was out at the time and the mudflats were a long way down. I would probably have been killed had they managed to heave me over, but they were stopped by two women who hit them with their handbags until they dropped me and legged it, laughing.

I hated the skinheads of my adolescence. I hated them. I also understood, vaguely, how Enoch Powell and the skins were committed to the same cause (an England cleansed of foreigners) though they used different means to bring it about. Powell, whose nasal accent I couldn't abide, provided the argument for a white United Kingdom (he did this with words, and, like reactionary Tories always do, he always maintained he spoke nothing but good old English common sense to which nobody could possibly take exception), while the skins provided the violence, the ultimate purpose of which was to drive immigrants out. Powell pretended there was no causality involved, and the thuggery (brutal, insouciant, terrifying, and I saw more than just the milk monitor bottled) was nothing to do with him. Wrong. It had everything to do with him, and in his faux denials my cynicism regarding politicians and their indefatigable capacity for dissembling first took root. Powell was the first politician I hated.

AFTON

A Fermanagh Wake (Sunday, 17 December 2006)

In my Irish summers with my grandparents in east Clare, labouring men were a regular feature on the roads, walking by the verge looking for a lift to work, to the shops, to their homes, and if we were out in a car (my grandparents didn't own one but a man in Tuamgraney with a Morris Oxford offered his services as a hackney) and we passed someone they recognised, Mr Mac would be asked to stop and a lift proffered. Invariably the offer would be accepted, and in would climb a man from O'Callaghan's Mills or Feakle, usually reeking of turf and woodsmoke. He would be full of gratitude, and as we drove on the passenger would talk and I would enter a sort of trance as I listened.

These memories date from the late fifties and early sixties of the last century. Since then Ireland changed. It joined the EU. It prospered. Its citizens (or some of them, at any rate) got richer, much richer. Cars became commonplace. In later years there were still hitchhikers, but mostly they were tourists. The working men, like those to whom my grandparents occasionally gave lifts, largely vanished, and it wasn't until I moved to County Fermanagh that I met the type again, the working person looking for a lift.

One was a woman, small and slight, early fifties, who had straw-coloured hair, always wore the same coat and carried her overalls and work shoes in a bulging plastic bag. I would see her on the Tempo Road in the early mornings when I was driving to the prison. Her technique with me and other drivers was never to put her thumb out but instead to flap her hand like a hanky to attract our attention. When she waved me down I always stopped. Then she would open the door and ask in her papery voice if I was going to Fivemiletown. I was always was going to Fivemiletown because it was on the way to Belfast and Maghaberry Prison. Once I confirmed I going to Fivemiletown she'd bundle herself in and buckle herself up. She was always punctilious about the safety belt. I would immediately notice the smell of turf and woodsmoke off her coat, exactly the same smell I remembered from childhood.

I'd press the accelerator. We would drive on. Nothing would be said. Not a word. We always drove in utter silence. That had been established the first time I gave her a lift. She didn't talk. We didn't talk. I didn't mind. It was too early for talking. When we got to the bakery where she worked, she would thank me in her papery voice, climb out and sidle through a plastic curtain on the other side of which, before I drove on, I sometimes glimpsed her fellow bakers in their workwear – hats, hairnets, white coats, Crocs, shoe covers. When I passed by the bakery in the evenings, going the other way, I would always look but I would never see her. I assumed her shift finished in the afternoon and someone must have picked her up and taken her back to wherever she went.

My other regular lift was a neighbour, Sinead. She lived – it is jarring and troubling to suddenly have to speak of her in the past tense – on a farm not far from the schoolhouse, with her husband and children. The UK may be a rich country, but in the late twentieth and early twenty-first centuries there is still a minority (certainly there is in Fermanagh) who live a carless life – the baker was one of this cohort and my neighbour Sinead was another. She didn't have a car. She'd never learnt to drive.

Her husband could drive and so could her son but they were often away, working down south or over in England, and whenever they were she had no alternative but to walk and so she did, she walked – to the houses round about where she worked as an occasional carer, to Enniskillen where she had a variety of cleaning jobs and where she also had to go for everything she needed: doctor, dentist, post office, supermarket. All the time and in all weathers, I would regularly see her out on the roads, beating along, and whenever I saw her I'd pick her up and take her on her way, and as we went she would talk without stopping about everybody and anybody in the area and their goings and comings. Her talk was genial, kind-hearted, tolerant, curious, and she never disparaged, and now this kind, good, cheerful, endlessly helpful, self-effacing woman who worked incredibly hard all her life has died, and as a neighbour, and as is customary, I went along, with my wife, to her wake.

In Fermanagh the open coffin at the wake is very much the tradition. When you go to a house for a wake, you know you are going to see the body. The London world I inhabited before I came to live here habitually recoiled from displaying the corpse and when, following my arrival in 1989, I attended my first funeral I was surprised to see the mourners sitting around the body, eating, drinking, talking, crying, reminiscing, children on their laps … But several further funerals have brought me to think that the open casket and the confrontation with death are healthy things. It's good for us to see the remains and to understand what awaits all of us at the end. The machine stops working and the beloved body becomes an inert mass, the lifelessness of which is palpable, because whatever it was that was there, consciousness, or the soul, or the spirit, or the spark, or whatever it was, or is, has gone, fled, who knows where. Knowing this is never going to make us worse; it may even make us better because it reminds us that we are finite and not immortal and, seeing as we are mortal, we'd better make the best use of the time we have remaining.

The wake for our neighbour was all day Sunday, and we arrived in the evening and were directed to a small curtained room. The open coffin was here, resting on red plastic chairs, the lid standing in the corner, keeping an eye on events. Our neighbour's face was heavily made-up while her hands, which in life were red, for in life she had been a hard-working woman, a veritable Stakhanovite, were coated with something that had given them such pallor and so smoothed their texture that for a moment I thought she was wearing gloves.

The husband, the widower, in new black shoes that squeaked and a new shirt made of a bright, stiff fabric (I imagined the wrapper in which it had come lying on his bed where he'd left it when he took the shirt out and got dressed earlier for the day), came and sat with us by the coffin, and as we stared at the corpse he told us what had happened.

His wife had noticed something was wrong in June. She had visited her doctor who was the useless Dr –, a byword for incompetence and about whom we already knew quite a bit, all bad. The doctor told her there was nothing to bother about. But there was something wrong. She knew her body. Things weren't right. So she went to the Erne hospital, many times, mostly to A&E. The nurses were unfriendly. 'Oh, look,' she overheard one saying to another once, 'she's back bothering us again.' Eventually she saw a consultant gynaecologist who diagnosed constipation. But the problems continued. She no longer had faith in the Erne Hospital (not after the remark she'd overheard) but the family had a friend who was a surgeon in Belfast. In August a biopsy was performed. Cancer was found, secondary, ovarian: the seat of the primary cancer couldn't be located. She began a course of treatment in Altnagelvin in Derry, as she wouldn't go back to the Erne. But it was too late. Her condition worsened. At the end of November she went into a side ward. At the start of December, she got something to stabilise the potassium in her blood. It made her nauseous and weak. She had died on the Friday just past.

As he told this horrible story, the widower had a piece of rolled-up paper in his hand, which he bent and twisted and tugged and folded obsessively. When he got to the end of his story, he mentioned how bleak Christmas was going to be without his wife, and as he did, he bent the little roll of paper he'd been fiddling with in two and tears filled his eyes. They came out of his eyes and then they got caught in the deep lines around his eyes.

His story finished, he went away to talk to the other mourners and we drank tea and ate digestive biscuits (the edges of which were melted because they had rested while on the saucer against the hot cup) and I had a nip of Paddy, rough and raw, another provoker of reveries, for in childhood it was one of the spirits I'd seen men drinking; and as we sat we looked at the body of our neighbour, who was no longer the woman we knew, her spirit having fled, leaving behind a version which was simultaneously like and not like her, in just the same way that the figures in Madame Tussauds are simultaneously like and not like the subjects they're supposed to represent.

An hour after we'd arrived, we left. Outside, a bitter wind was blowing. It was pitch-black and there was frost on the ground. Our conversation as we slithered home was bleak and angry. Our neighbour was a working-class woman whose social status, according to our ridiculous caste system, was low and, as a result, she had no or little clout. Symptomatic in June, she was dead by December. In six months, she had gone from life to death. It was quick and brutal and the speed and the brutality had everything to do with her place in society – it would have been a completely different story had she come from a different class. A middle-class woman would perhaps not have been shooed away by the doctor or denigrated by the nurses in the local hospital. Had she been a middle-class woman, she might even still be alive. We like to tell ourselves that in this very rich country the old inequalities have been done away with, but that is a delusion.

They haven't. The truth is that outcomes, especially health outcomes, are often determined by social class, and good health is often in direct ratio to wealth. The poor die earlier. That's the kind of country we live in and it is nothing to be proud of, my wife and I agreed. Nothing. There was nothing else to say. We hurried on, the schoolhouse in the distance, lights twinkling. We'd banked the stove before leaving, and once we were home we'd soon warm up.

H.M.P. MAZE
POSSESSION OF
A MEANS OF
IDENTIFICATION

A Long Day (Thursday, 25 January 2007)

I went to bed on Wednesday night and was still awake as the hands of my alarm clock reached midnight and Thursday began. One reason I couldn't sleep was Pat Ramsey, the publisher of Lagan Press, had telephoned at lunchtime on Wednesday to say he'd publish my 'prison novel' *A Good Day for a Dog*; the other reason was Thomas Fee, a lifer with whom I'd had an encounter in Maghaberry earlier in the week.

We go back a long way, me and Mr Fee. I first met him ten years ago, when I was starting in Maghaberry. Shortly after I arrived he was released on life licence. I heard reports of his progress over the years. He was doing okay, he was making a life. Then, some time last year, calamity: he had been arrested in England and bounced back to Maghaberry. Several months after his ignominious return, Thomas sent me a message. He needed help with his writing. Would I call to see him? And Monday, at the start of the week, that's what I did.

It was evening, during association (the period when prisoners are unlocked and allowed to socialise), when I appeared at his cell door. I saw Thomas inside lying on his bed. The curtains over the barred window were pulled against the dark night.

I said hello from the threshold – I never enter a cell without permission – and Thomas got up. His body was long and lanky, and he had a medieval face the colour of ivory and a haircut to match. He also looked terrible – shocked, cowed, beaten.

He told me to come in. I did. The cell (I took this in with a single glance) was bleak and impersonal. Thomas's cell's furnishings, besides the bed, consisted of a plastic chair, a rickety table and an open wardrobe. In the corner was a sink with toiletries on the edge (prison-issue 'Welcome Pack' toothpaste, shaving soap, razor, toothbrush) and, behind a modesty screen, a stainless-steel toilet. There were no personal touches, although Thomas had been back for months, because Thomas was a man who, at this time in his life, had no relationships, no outside contacts, no family connections, nothing. He was untethered socially; thus, he had nobody who would give him even a photograph. And he got no visits either. He was completely alone. In terms of size (all the more obvious because it was so empty) the cell was two paces from the steel cell door to the window and six foot across. I could just about touch the two side walls standing in the middle of the floor with my arms stretched out. The cell smelt of fish batter and Harpic.

Thomas offered the plastic chair and gave me his lumpy prison-issue pillow to sit on. He perched on his hard mattress, which sat on the metal prison-issue bed frame that was screwed to the floor to stop it being used in a riot as a barricade. We exchanged pleasantries. How long since I had last seen him? Years. I'd met him in 1997 and then he was already an old lag with years behind him … and now he was an even older old lag … oh my Lord, how time flew. Overhead the neon strip whined and fizzed, while outside, on the landing, beyond the open door, the clack of pool balls, the rumble of male voices, prisoners enjoying their rough pleasures …

Thomas's father grew up in a Cork orphanage, his mother in poverty in County Kerry. They married and had a lot of children, double figures. In the fifties, the Fees moved to the north of Ireland in search of work (a horrible experience – they were Catholics, they didn't prosper) and then to the north of England, where they settled in Leeds.

Thomas's earliest memories were of their family home being endlessly raided by the police. All his older brothers and his father were criminals. As a child, Thomas spent a lot of time in care and foster homes. Once he was out of the care system, Thomas became a petty career criminal. As an adolescent he was arrested and convicted frequently. He was sent to an approved school, then borstal. In his early twenties, he committed what he called his index offence (I presume he picked up the phrase from a prison psychologist): he broke into a house and murdered the householder who wouldn't tell him where his money was hidden and was sentenced to twenty years – though as things turned out, he served many years more than the tariff. Thomas was an unruly prisoner: he was endlessly in trouble and endlessly charged (put on report and sent to the punishment block) and endlessly ghosted from one jail to another in the middle of the night, so nobody knew where he was. He lost contact with his family. Some years into his sentence, in a prison in the south of England, he discovered Buddhism and meditation and, through a Church of England vicar, he met Margaret, a Christian, and fell in love.

Thomas eventually transferred to Northern Ireland and got out, settling with Margaret outside Omagh. He established himself as a market gardener (with some success), though he found socialising difficult and in social situations couldn't keep intrusive thoughts out of his mind, couldn't stop remembering the violent things he'd done and the violent things done to him in English jails by officers and prisoners. Thomas's oddness and his social difficulties were problematic for Margaret; they drifted apart and eventually the relationship broke down. Thomas left their home and moved into a horrible flat in a horrible block in

Cookstown. He started drinking. One evening the police visited him. They'd received an anonymous letter about his violent criminal past and his deeds while in jail (attacking prison officers and other prisoners, long periods in solitary), written, he presumed, by a fellow tenant who had been supplied with these details by a 'friend' in the prison service. The policemen who visited Thomas put him on notice. They were watching him, they said. He'd better behave, and if he didn't they'd come down on him like a ton of bricks and whisk him back to prison so fast his feet wouldn't touch the ground.

Thomas, being Thomas, pre-empted the inevitable and fled – where else? – to Leeds, where he'd not been in decades but where he still had family. At first, amazingly, things were okay. He stayed with his oldest brother, also a criminal, whom he hadn't spoken to since the 1980s. One evening he went to see another brother, a criminal and also a schizophrenic. Thomas and the second brother drank, argued and fought. Then they patched things up. Thomas fell asleep on the sofa. At four in the morning, several policemen woke him. First, they beat him, then they carted him off to Leeds police station. Here he found out what had happened: the second brother had left the house while he was sleeping, gone to the police station and told the sergeant behind the desk that his flat had been taken over by a dangerous man who'd thrown him out.

After two days in the police cells, Thomas was up before the magistrate: the charges (trespass, resisting arrest, 'Mickey Mouse' stuff, he called it) were thrown out. However, the Leeds police had been onto Maghaberry Prison. His recall was being set in motion, although he would not discover this just yet.

Released by the court he went into Leeds town centre – and here the story got very odd. Thomas went to a pub and drank three pints. His drinks, he believed, were spiked, for next thing he was asleep in the middle of the city and a policeman was waking him up. He was taken to the station, charged with being drunk and disorderly and resisting arrest. The next morning, he applied for bail, but this was denied because his recall for licence breach was now in train and the police objected to bail as he was a flight risk. He was remanded to HMP Doncaster (one of these new private prisons where you buy everything, even a mirror to shave with, as he observed glumly). He spent two months at Doncaster, then was transferred to HMP Manchester, where he spent one night. The morning following, he was taken to Manchester airport, flown, cuffed to his escort, to Aldergrove and returned to Maghaberry, where the Life Sentence Review Commissioners ruled he must receive therapy in order to help him regulate his behaviour and drinking, and until that happened he would not be considered for release.

This was months ago but, despite this ruling, nothing had happened as yet. His fear was that nothing would happen and that when he next went up before the commissioners and they discovered nothing had happened, another year or two would be added on and this might well go on for years ... So given the system wouldn't or couldn't help him (he did concede resources in the prison were stretched, and there were insufficient therapists in the prison to do the work with prisoners that needed to be done), he had therefore concluded the only thing he could do to achieve what he puzzlingly called 'catheris' – which I eventually realised was catharsis – was to help himself. And, boiled down to essentials, that meant writing the story of his life. By doing this, he believed he would achieve what a course of therapy would.

When I heard this, I felt alarmed. Writing can be therapeutic, I agreed, and indeed a therapist might recommend writing an account of traumatic events as part of the therapeutic process – but writing alone, without the input of a therapist, would not help him to regulate his behaviour. It couldn't do what therapy does. He had to lower his expectations, I said. He should think of writing not as a cure but as a practice, which, one, would give pleasure; two, would be outside the purview of the prison authorities and so would be entirely his own and have nothing to do with them; three, would boost confidence; four, would stimulate memory (prisoners often complain incarceration causes loss of brain function – they're right, it does – and writing, I know, is one way of resisting and even retarding atrophy); and five, would pass the time in a useful and meaningful way. And then, when therapy began, he would have something for the therapist to read that would offer some insight into what he sprang from.

I also emphasised writing something good took work and time, to which Thomas answered he was a grafter and he had plenty of time. We talked then about his chaotic infancy and early boyhood (one of his earliest memories was learning, aged three, how to spring the caps off beer bottles for his father and his criminal friends at their all-night drinking sessions in the family home; he got a ha'penny for every bottle he opened) and how to go about getting this kind of incendiary content written down. Of course, he would want the words to come out straight and neat, but if he forced them to come straight and neat they would lose the savour, texture and the feeling of his lived experience. He had to let the words tumble out and fall onto the page in whatever shape and order they wished, I said, and he had to leave the tidying up and the technical stuff till later. I recommended Hugh Collins' *Autobiography of a Murderer* as the best memoir of a criminal's chaotic childhood that I knew of. I promised I would obtain a copy and lend it to him, and I said I would see him in a week's time and we would read together what he had written. And then I left, with my head reeling.

Lying in bed last night, unable to sleep, hearing the clock's mechanism murmuring as the second hand swept round the face, I found myself unable to stop thinking about Thomas. He has done huge damage and he is himself hugely damaged and rectification will be the work of years, assuming he can even get help; more than likely he won't, because the resources simply aren't there – either in the criminal justice system or in society.

And when I wasn't thinking about Thomas I was thinking about my novel, which attempts to communicate with a narrative the story of someone who, like Thomas, does terrible things; the novel attempts to explain why this is so by showing how this character doesn't choose to do harm but rather can't choose not to do harm because he is himself so damaged. But how can a novel, I thought, compete with facts like those Thomas had given me? His life story completely outclassed my inventions. Once again, the perennial problem: when set against reality, fiction so often seems thinner.

I did fall asleep eventually and I woke to find every blade of grass and every twig outside was coated in white frost. I drove my middle son to his grammar school on hard, bone-dry roads. On the way home, I stopped at the post office and sent off the manuscript of *A Good Day for a Dog* to Hazel Orme, the copy editor. It felt good, just one day after the call from the publisher, to be doing this.

I spent the morning at my desk. At one o'clock the secretary from the Model Primary School rang. My youngest son had been in a collision with another boy and taken to casualty.

I set off for the hospital: the gears, having been fine earlier, now were mysteriously troublesome … In the hospital, I found my son in a waiting room. He had a vast bandage wrapped around his head. The teaching assistant beside him assured me there was nothing I need worry about. I found it hard to hear her as my attention was transfixed by the great black patches of blood on my son's school jumper.

My wife arrived. I drove the teaching assistant back to school and returned. Both journeys had to be made in third gear. Why was it today of all days that the gearbox had decided to die?

In the hospital, my son had been moved to an examination couch. The bandage was off. At the bottom of the gash over his right eye I could see a terrifying line of white bone. A nurse called Sharon ran various tests and then a second nurse, Cathal, arrived with suturing needles and thread. He drew on plastic gloves. I saw his wedding ring through the material. He injected local anaesthetic and then began to push the suturing needle in for the first stitch. My son cried out.

Sharon leant forward. 'Do you have any pets, darling?'

'Yes,' he shouted.

'Is it a dog?'

'Yes.'

'What kind of doggie is it?'

'It's fifty-seven varieties, a Heinz dog,' he said. 'Now, please, go away. I don't want to talk to you.'

Behind the needle the thread was pulling through. My wife was pale and also green … and I – crikey! I wasn't smirking, was I? Yes, I was! It was my son's answers. They made me want to laugh (I always want to laugh when I hear authority getting lip), but as I couldn't laugh I had to smirk instead. Which is worse.

The first stitch was tied off and the needle went in for the second stitch. My wife put her head between her knees. My son moaned.

'What did you get for Christmas, darling?' Sharon asked.

'Go away,' my son said. 'I don't want to talk to you.'

My smirk was spreading and hardening. I covered my face, hoping to give the impression of a father in distress when actually what I was really doing was hiding my expression so no one would see it.

'You know Cathal doesn't mean to hurt you,' I heard the nurse say.

'But he is,' said my son. 'Now, please, go away, I don't want to talk to you.'

Three more stitches and the job was done. I dropped my hands and watched as the wound was dressed. I was given some information sheets on delayed concussion and told to check on my son every three hours while he was sleeping. *Did they notice me smirking? I hope not*, I thought.

'It's a miracle I didn't pass out,' I heard my wife murmuring as she lifted her head. 'I was sure I was going to.'

We went home. We were exhausted. Our son, in contrast, was his old ebullient self – throwing himself about, happy as Larry. I took the car to the garage. Besides the clutch, the water pump had also packed up; new headlight bulbs were needed too. Repairs would run to hundreds.

My son was having his ninth birthday party at Laser Quest on Sunday afternoon. However, with six stitches we obviously couldn't risk him running around in the dark for an hour and having another collision. My wife spent the evening ringing round all the invitees and cancelling.

The Irish in England (Thursday, 9 October 2008)

A day with the Irish in England, both varieties – those who kick with the wrong foot and those who kick with right foot, a distinction which derives from the figure of speech 'He digs with the wrong foot'. This way of distinguishing between Catholic and Protestant owed its origins to the tradition of left- and right-handed spades in Irish agriculture and the notion that Catholics could always be identified because of their spade preference. Which the Catholic foot is I've never quite understood: in the north it's the left, I think, but in the south, my friends there tell me, it's Protestants who are the left-footers. Such are the arcane details that underpin sectarian animus.

In the morning I went by train from Liverpool Street station to a town out in Essex for the funeral of Elizabeth, the wife of an old friend. The church was a Catholic church. The deceased was a Catholic, from a family of Irish Catholics.

The post-war Irish emigrants who went to England typically arrived as singletons, met an Irish partner, married and then moved to a place where they could raise children. Elizabeth was part of that cohort. Her parents had come to London from rural Ireland in the late 1940s. After they met and married, they settled in Essex. They chose the town because it had an Irish club and an Irish community and Catholic schools. There was a church, but the congregation they joined built a new one in the 1960s, and it was in this new church that the funeral Mass was heard. The atmosphere of the church, no surprise really, was very much Irish rather than Anglo-Catholic: Irish names and Irish accents and Irish-themed notices everywhere (about the GAA, coaches to Ireland, that sort of thing), all of which suggested to me that these parishioners were still in touch with the place from which they, or more likely their forebears, sprang. The priest, Father F–, hailed from Galway. He was garrulous and overfamiliar, endlessly rolling his eyes and winking at mourners as if to say, 'I feel your pain, really, I do …' and he spoke in a booming theatrical manner, like an Irish Brian Blessed. (I couldn't keep my eyes off him, as I knew he would make great copy.) The priest was assisted by a portly and noisy lay churchman, Irish again, deferential, forelock-tugging and very much Madge to the priest's Dame Edna. It was just like being in Ireland, really, but about fifty years ago …

The service over, we adjourned to an Essex pub full of blokes in England football tops watching Millwall reruns on the widescreen TV. Talk among the mourners was of the Mass and Catholicism and, oh goodness, the debates were feisty and loud and prolonged. There were four camps, each proposing, advancing and defending different points of view. By far the largest group was composed of the English friends of the deceased. These people were metropolitan, educated, cultured and, by and large, not religious. They were appalled by the things the priest had said about Jesus and the love of God, the afterlife and heaven. Interestingly, this group, even as they recoiled in horror, were not unhappy to have their disapproval of organised religion in general and Catholicism in particular confirmed by what they had seen. They relished being appalled.

The next-largest group was friends who'd travelled from Ireland who weren't believers either, for the most part, but who tried to explain to the first group that they'd missed the point and that the service wasn't for them:

the service was for believers, those who had faith, and if they weren't of that number, so what? They should just let those for whom it was intended, the faithful, derive benefit from it and stop with the carping.

The third group was the family of the deceased, who were Catholics and Irish or of Irish descent: these were the people for whom the service offered comfort and succour.

The fourth group was the smallest, and it comprised just one person, the professional fence-sitter – me. I am not a believer (and happily concede Catholicism is appalling, even though I will also take communion … what ho, Pascal's wager and all that – you can always count on me to cover all the bases), yet at the same time I could see what the service had done for those with faith. I am a Janus facing in two directions. Catholicism is bunkum but I can also see that for the suffering relatives of the deceased (a beautiful woman who died far too young) the service performed a miracle: it made the situation bearable or manageable or something. It took the sting out of her death – perhaps that's the way to put it.

In the evening I went to Stansted to catch a plane to Belfast. Here I met the other kind of Irish – the ones who kicked with the right foot, if it's Catholics who use the left foot in the north, that is. My plane was delayed that evening and, along with everyone else on the flight, I had to wait. It is never good to have to wait, but the experience was made worse by the fact that at Gate 87 in Stansted there are only about twelve seats. (I'm exaggerating, but only a bit.) This meant the majority, myself included, had to sit on the floor. This group included a mob of young soldiers returning from basic training, in Colchester probably, who talked loudly (and hilariously) about the British army NCOs who'd supervised them.

'My sergeant,' said one, 'you know what he said to me at kit inspection this morning?'

Another soldier shook his head. 'No,' he said. 'What did he say?'

Everyone was looking and listening, not only the other young soldiers but also me.

'He says to me, "You're from Portadown, aren't you?" I say, "I am."

'"I was bricked by fucking rioters when I was there," he says. "How old are you?"

I tell him. "Oh, right," he says, "well, that would make you just the right age for when I was bricked. Were you one of those cunts who bricked me?"

"No, no, not me, sergeant," I say. "I wouldn't have thrown a brick at a Brit. I'm a Prod. I'm loyal. And I'm the in army now, aren't I? 'Course I didn't brick you, sarge."

"Is that right?" he says. "Well, you're still a fucking Paddy, so don't give me any of your Irish crap. You're all cunts, you hear? All you Irish are cunts … Now, what did I say?"

"I'm a cunt?" I say.

"No, you're not listening, Paddy. I didn't say that. I said all you Irish are cunts, you and the rest, every one of you."

"I hear you, sarge," I say, "all you Irish are cunts. How 'bout I spell it, prove I really got it? A-l-l-y-o-u-i-r-i-s-h … Oh no, I'm stuck … Help me out, sarge – you know this I'm sure … how do you spell cunts?" All the lads on kit inspection are cracking up now.

"Shut up, Paddy," shouts the sarge. He's fucking steaming. He knows he's had the piss taken. He's just not quite sure how. "Shut up, shut the fuck up." Off he stomps …' And here the soldier jumped up and imitated his sergeant's heavy-footed retreat.

The other soldiers now took it in turns to tell similar stories which demonstrated that the English NCOs had no understanding of Northern Ireland, nor anything good to say about the Northern Irish recruits. Yet none of the recruits, as far as I could tell, felt bitter or disgruntled at what had been said to them during training. Nor did the recruits feel slighted by the disdain or the casual racism of the English NCOs (which, no doubt, they saw in the barracks was nothing in comparison to what those with black skins endured); on the contrary, what they took from the experience was that these exchanges proved their NCOs, and by inference the English, were too dim to understand the complexities of Ulster society and the identification of its Protestant citizens with the British state. Furthermore, these soldiers seemed to quite enjoy the way the NCOs proved what idiots they were every time they opened their mouths. Perhaps, like their left-foot-kicking compatriots (who definitely know the English are completely ignorant when it comes to the complexities of Ireland), these raw recruits enjoyed the lovely frisson of superiority which surely follows every exchange between a slippery and mischievous Irishman and an obdurate and dense Englishman.

Eventually the flight was announced. As we all rose to our feet I felt, for once, I hadn't wasted my time while I'd been kept waiting at an airport.

The Death of a Childhood Friend (Friday, 23 January 2009)

The phone went. 'Are you Carlo Gébler?'

The speaker was English, but I couldn't place her. 'Yes.'

'I'm Karen.'

I was still none the wiser.

'I'm Peter Robinson's wife.'

Ah, Peter Robinson. The name was an iceberg's tip sticking above the ocean while below, out of sight, was the iceberg's bulk and a wealth of memory. When I was a child and we lived at 257 Cannon Hill Lane, Morden, Mr and Mrs Robinson, who had three children, were our neighbours and lived a few doors down the hill. Mr Robinson worked for a company that built roads, and every morning he set off for work wearing a bowler hat and carrying a briefcase and a rolled umbrella. He had lost a finger in the war (memory says he was in the artillery but I might be wrong) so he wore a prosthetic glove, and if he saw me in the morning, he would wave with his mysterious gloved hand in my direction and I always felt a thrill when he did. Then he would cross Cannon Hill Lane to the common and clip away, moving at an incredible pace (he walked even faster than my parents, both of whom were formidable walkers) towards Raynes Park railway station, where he caught the train into London. Mrs Robinson was kind, gentle, patient, always wore an apron, spoke quietly and listened carefully. Of the first-born son I have little recollection. I suspect he'd left home by 1958, when we arrived. He was a mysterious figure who came and went (I did occasionally glimpse him), a young man, out in the world, who wore sharp suits and good ties and was aloof and unavailable but also appealing in the way young men who were making their way in the world were, at least to me. I was a lonely boy and I longed for a mysterious, aloof young man to make me his friend and show me the ways of the world. But the oldest Robinson was not that person.

The second Robinson was Annie. I don't think I ever spoke to her. She was beautiful and wore long floaty dresses – at least, that's what I remember her wearing – and she went about the common – or so I heard, I never saw this myself – *in her bare feet.* I found the notion terrifying. Bare feet! This put her in the same category as the ranting solitaries (high on methylated spirits, it was always said) whom I sometimes came across on the common or outside Morden underground station. It put her outside the herd, it made her a focus of hostility, and I wanted nothing to do with someone like that. I was not just a conformist: I lacked courage.

At the same time, I found Annie's barefootedness thrilling and exciting. Though I wouldn't have been able to put this into words back then, I believed her nonconforming was an act of heroism. You had to say no, as I dimly realised, to the culture of our torpid suburban streets, but no one apart from Annie seemed to be doing this.

The youngest of our neighbours was the one I knew best; this was Peter. We were the same age. We went to Hillcross Primary School, or at least for two years we did, and every morning I called to his house and we walked together to school, and every afternoon we met at the school gate and we walked back to Cannon Hill Lane, which was a lot of time to spend together, though I can't remember anything of it. His sister, though we hardly had any contact, made a far greater impression.

I do have other odd Robinson memories. Once I had to sleep in the Robinsons' house, I don't remember why – were my parents on holiday, and where was my brother? – and I was put to bed in the older brother's room, which as it happened was the back bedroom, the same as my own bedroom at home. In the corner I noticed a pair of boots, heavy brown walking boots with silver eyes and thick intestinal-coloured laces, fat spongy soles and great lewd tongues that stuck out from under the laces in a rude and offensive and threatening manner. On seeing these boots, I was seized by the idea that they were animated by a malevolent spirit that had me in its sights, and that as soon as I fell asleep, these terrible boots would come to life. They would fly across the room and fall on me with ferocious force. They would pulverise my frame. They would drive the air from my lungs. They would bruise my face and break my fingers. They would stamp me to death. At the certain knowledge of what awaited should I fall asleep (or even, I feared, if I just closed my eyes), I was seized by uncontrolled terror and I began to howl and shriek.

My cries were heard by Mrs Robinson. She came in wearing her apron, smelling of soap, bent down so her eyeline was level with my eyeline and asked me in her quiet, reasonable voice what the matter was. I told her. It was the boots. Should I fall asleep, should I even close my eyes, they would fly at me, trample me, kick me, savage me, do away with me, for they were killer boots informed by the spirit of who knew what.

The next part of this saga is a blank. Perhaps I was put in Peter's room. Or perhaps the boots were taken away. But whatever was the case is lost.

My other strong memory, and here I have a conclusion, is of a birthday party, Peter's fifth or sixth – a 1950s birthday party: paper hats, crackers, vividly coloured balloons strung everywhere, bunting across the doorways and around the ceiling edges of the back dining room;

girls in shimmering frocks and patent sandals, boys in their good shorts and their best shoes; games (beautifully supervised by Mrs Robinson but, alas, not the sister, Annie) of Pass the Parcel, Blind Man's Buff, Pin the Tail on the Donkey and Are You There, Mr Wolf?

And then the tea, eaten off the table in the dining room with a tablecloth: platters of sandwiches (white bread, crusts cut off, cucumber, fish paste, ham and cheese) and cakes and brightly coloured jellies, rounded off (before the cake) with, treat of treats, tinned pineapple and tinned cream. I had never eaten either. I shovelled the food in, the fruit sticky and oversweet, the cream glutinous, rubbery, and immediately knew I was going to be violently sick. I sprinted through the French doors at the dining room's rear, scrambled to the nearest flower bed and vomited all over Mr Robinson's beautiful rose bushes, coating the beautiful pink petals and the waxy green leaves and the thick thorny stems with my sick that was a mix of jellies, cakes, sandwiches, yellow pulpy pineapple chunks and white gooey tinned cream.

In September 1960, Peter went off to prep school to be prepared to sit the Common Entrance examination. The Robinsons belonged to a caste above us, and I had no idea what that caste was or any understanding of its rituals or that it had a different schooling system to the state system in which I was swimming; all this understanding came later. I don't remember Peter going and nor do I remember whether we acknowledged one another whenever our paths crossed thereafter.

Forty years after these events I came to write about those times and the life I lived in Cannon Hill Lane, and in the course of researching and writing the book eventually published as *Father & I*, my cousin Clancy Gébler-Davies mentioned she knew someone from that life I'd lived as a child: it was Peter Robinson. She said he might help me with the book and gave me his number.

On Tuesday, 19 October 1999, I phoned Peter. The voice at the other end of the line, not heard for forty years, was quiet and reasonable. That was his mother's legacy, perhaps. He was a social worker, child protection. I mentioned the book and its subject, my difficult relationship with my father. He didn't seem surprised I was writing about this.

'You had the most miserable expression of any child I ever met,' he said. 'You were so unhappy.' He remembered visiting our house. 'The atmosphere was very odd,' he said. 'It wasn't pleasant. It wasn't child-friendly.'

We moved on to his memories of the area, and he told me how he was once kidnapped by Teddy boys on Cannon Hill Common. He was taken into the bushes and someone stubbed a cigarette out on his hand.

He agreed to read the manuscript. I sent it.

On Saturday, 27 November 1999, Peter Robinson rang. He had marked up the manuscript and would return it. He had spotted all sorts of little errors which could be easily rectified. He also noted I had made no mention of the two years we had walked to and from school together, but that was also, he added, a characteristic of memoir, which was a record not of fact but of what was recalled. I wanted to know what he thought of the book as a narrative, as a literary artefact. He thought it was all right.

'You have your father's voice,' he said. 'It's strange, more than strange, to think of everything you describe going on just a few doors from where we lived.'

'Do you ever go back?'

'Where – to Cannon Hill Lane?'

'Yes,' I said.

'I went back ten years ago.'

'And?'

'Everything's smaller, diminished,' he said. 'I wouldn't recommend it.'

From the memory of that conversation I came back to the present, to the phone I was holding in my hand and to the woman at the other end of the line, who had introduced herself as Peter's wife, Karen Robinson.

'You're not going to tell me something has happened to Peter,' I said.

Haltingly, her voice plangent and even tearful, Karen told me he had been diagnosed last July with cancer. Secondaries had been found. The primary was never found. He had been incredibly brave, incredibly brave, had never complained once and, yes, she had rung to tell me the worst. Yes, he had died.

I put down the phone and then didn't move on account of the memories teeming; the early mornings in Cannon Hill Lane (this was after Peter went off to prep school), emptying the anthracite ash into the bin at the front (my chore was to relight the fire in the back dining room every morning before school, so every day started with the ritual emptying of the bitter-smelling coarse-grained ash) and seeing Mr Robinson swinging out his gate in his bowler hat, seeing him wave (sometimes), hearing him call 'Good morning' (sometimes), and watching him crossing the road to the common and speeding away in the direction of the railway station; the common itself, with its paths and great oaks and muddy playing fields with their white lines of flaking paint and goalposts with sagging nets which smelt of fish (that was the odour when the twine began to rot), where teams thumped heavy balls on Sunday mornings, while ranks of supporters shouted abuse and puffed on their fags; the dank, shallow pond at the lower end of the common, where fishermen sat for hours watching their floats and occasionally hooked fat tench and perch that would be weighted to applause from other fishermen before being thrown back into the dark waters; the island in the middle of the pond, home to angry swans whose wings, when they flexed them, sounded like creaking leather; the lightning-blasted oak in front of our house where the open-air cinema truck parked some Sundays and where I saw *Whistle Down the Wind* and fell in love with its star, Hayley Mills; and finally, bigger than all these other memories put together, the clanking and clattering sounds, from first thing in the morning on waking to last thing at night on falling asleep, of trains shunting up and down the Wimbledon line, rackety, clackety, rackety, clackety.

And living as he had, I now thought, a few doors away from my house, my friend Peter must have heard the same rackety-clackety. It was a sound that had entered my bones and never left. Had it entered his? I should have asked him when I had the chance.

H.R.H.PRINC
WALES

Hanging with the Apprentice Boys (Saturday, 4 December 2010)

There is looming in the future (courtesy of DoubleBand Films) the possibility of presenting and writing for television a history of the siege of Derry on the foot of my book *The Siege of Derry*, and for this reason I spent two days in the Maiden City with a crew and a director.

Our plan was to film, on the Friday, the commemoration of the shutting of the city's gates in 1688 by apprentice boys (which kept Lord Antrim's Catholic redshanks out) by modern-day admirers (members of the Apprentice Boys of Derry, a Protestant fraternal society), some in costume, who every year march from gate to gate on the same day the original apprentice boys had. Then the following day, Saturday, we'd film the annual burning of the effigy of Colonel Robert Lundy (the Scottish Episcopalian governor of Derry and suspected closet Jacobite, who it is believed would have handed Derry to the Catholics and who remains to this day a Judas figure to loyalists). Our hope is that all this material, once edited into a pilot, will be so brilliant broadcasters will want to shower us with money.

My Friday evening started in the Apprentice Boys' Memorial Hall (in the bar, to be precise). It was filled with drunken bandsmen, Northern Irish and Scottish, and their women. Their faces, their bodies, were positively seventeenth century even if their clothes weren't. And they were joshing, sparring, courting, kicking, shoving, pushing, dancing and singing along to the DJ's tunes, an eclectic mix of Kasabian, Rangers F.C. songs and horrible nineteenth-century ballads about killing Catholics.

At midnight, with several Apprentice Boys dressed in period costume (Ulster intransigence meets am-dram), we went onto the walls for the ceremonial firing of the cannon, which signals the start of proceedings. The event was watched by a lively crowd of bandsmen and Apprentice Boys singing 'Rule Britannia' and 'I Was Born under an Ulster Star' (to the tune of 'I Was Born under a Wandering Star').

Then we slithered through the icy, snowy streets with a group of bandsmen for the touching of the gates: it consists of literally that, one man after another touching a gate with religious reverence. We accompanied the votaries to Butcher's Gate and Bishop's Gate, but we couldn't go any further with them. Republican Sinn Féin or the 32 County Sovereignty Movement (or somebody with an over-elaborate name) was at Ferry Quay and Ship Quay Gate (mounting a counter event) and trouble was expected, they said, and they didn't want the camera damaged. Or perhaps they didn't want us filming the boys scrapping with the Fenians – a distinct possibility, for news of impending trouble and looming violence was communicated with barely concealed delight. Oh, how we love a riot! Always up for a ruck in Nordern Ireland, we are. We took the news in good heart (being middle class, myself and crew, obviously we didn't want to riot) and slunk back to the hotel (my goodness, it was icy and cold in Derry, verging on the inhuman) and went to bed.

Saturday morning, we were back at the Apprentice Boys' Memorial Hall very early to watch the Lundy effigy (enormous, at least twenty-foot high and incredibly heavy) being trundled on a gibbet with wheels to Society Street, where it would be burnt later on. I had to do various bits to camera, watched by bandsmen. It was a miracle they didn't pelt us with snowballs. Then we filmed bands and Apprentice Boys marching around the frosty foggy streets (very atmospheric). Passing the Apprentice Boys' Memorial Hall, all the marchers pointed with their left hands at the door as a mark of respect and, like the gate-touching the night before, it seemed sacred: the bands were watched by a small but enthusiastic crowd (though I did notice here and there some lantern-jawed men with harps, Celtic crosses and other suspect symbols tattooed on their hands who were not clapping – obviously the other kind up from the Bogside to gawp at the enemy). Overall, however, the atmosphere was welcoming and genial. The crowds were mostly rural people from west of the Bann, and their demeanour – raucous, ribald and drunken, genial, friendly and bumptious – wasn't remotely like that of your Belfast loyalist, who tends to the hostile, curmudgeonly and flinty. Of course, I still wouldn't have wanted to have had an argument with any of these people about the importance of an ecumenical approach to Irish affairs – these were all Prod triumphalists – but they didn't have the edge, the menace or the vitriol of their hardened Belfast kin. They were here to party, and they were happy to have anyone who wanted to join in join in, even a film crew.

The day ended with everyone (maybe five thousand people) gathered round the Lundy effigy, which had a placard on the front reading 'Robert Lundy' and one on the back reading 'The fate of all traitors'. (Colonel Lundy, so the story goes, would have betrayed the city to the Catholics only his Proddy compatriots, wary and beady-eyed, first slammed the gates to keep out Lord Antrim's Catholic redshanks, and second stopped Lundy admitting James II when he turned up outside Derry asking to be let in. Yep, Lundy was a wrong 'un, allegedly, but the Prods had his number, and now they burn his effigy to remind themselves to never let their guard down – this is the important bit

– because there are traitors everywhere who are out to trample you into the mud.)

As all the bands played together – the noise was incredible: there were maybe thirty bands, and the crowds jeered and sang and cavorted and danced drunkenly around, a Bruegel scene – Lundy was set alight. Think *The Wicker Man* because, oh yes, this was a pagan expiation as much as it was an historical commemoration. The effigy was filled with paraffin so it roared into flame, and the crowds roared their approval as this symbol of seventeenth-century disloyalty went up in smoke. After ten minutes the effigy was gone (given the incredible build-up, the climax was over pretty quick – blink and you'd miss it) and everyone began to drift back to the clapped-out touring coaches that had brought them all to Derry that morning and which were parked down by the Fountain estate and outside the walls. As the crowds washed away, I met an official from the Apprentice Boys whom I'd met briefly the night before. He wore a suit, a tie, had a lovely Ulster brogue. He was a friendly, classy, civilised kind of guy. He liked his literature, especially Heaney. He liked his Irish whiskey. He liked Dublin. He thought Catholics had a raw deal when Stormont was in charge. He thought the Good Friday Agreement was a good thing. He was the kind of bourgeois bastion with whom it really wouldn't be too bad having dinner. Well, I had my speech prepared and here, delivered by the kindly Fates, was the very man to deliver it to. I cleared my throat.

'Lundy wasn't a traitor,' I said. 'Or a Catholic. He was a Scottish Episcopalian and he swore an oath to William of Orange. Terrible man-management skills, of course, and he was very annoying, plus tactless and charmless. But he was never a traitor. He was never going to turn the city over to James.'

My listener smiled. 'Of course,' he said. He removed his hat and put it back on again. Obviously, it was a bowler. I'd never met a man who took his bowler off and on like this.

'He was just an unlucky man,' the bowler-hatted one continued, 'who was in a tight spot, but try telling that to …' He gestured at the bandsmen around us.

Agreed, I thought. *It would be a complete waste of time to tell the truth about Lundy to this crowd. Of course, of course.* But no sooner was this thought out than the next followed.

We all had our myths that we thought of as truths, and we were all loath either to give them up or to listen to anyone who wanted to put us straight about them, and I was no different in that respect from anyone else …

After all, didn't everything I'd thought over the previous twenty-four hours, about the people among whom I'd been swimming and whose rites and rituals I'd been watching, have its own mythical underpinning?

It wasn't their truth I saw in the commemoration of the closing of the gates (beleaguered people celebrate the moment when they saved themselves from extinction) but mine (insecure colonists celebrate the moment they retreated behind the high walls they'd constructed to protect themselves from the aggrieved and uppity natives whom they'd completely screwed and who were quite justifiably enraged). Hundreds of years on from 1688, the kith and kin of the gate-slammers were still feeling threatened (the recent Troubles had been remarkably helpful in that respect) and so were carrying on carrying on with their No Surrender schtick – and, incidentally, sticking to the tried-and-tested Irish mantra 'To hell with the future, my friends, let's get on with the past!' – but I was sticking to my schtick and mine was different to theirs. In my eyes these crowds were the descendants of the oppressing class, and my sympathies were with the other kind, the oppressed, whose descendants had Irish harps tattooed on the backs of their hands and who came up from the Bogside to gawp. We make nicey-nicey but we all float in our version of the truth.

The pilot will be cut this week and sent to the BBC and others and then we wait. I feel quite sanguine about this. I know television is very fickle; I know all broadcasters are capricious and I've no expectation we will get a yes. It's a relief to feel indifferent. Actually, it isn't indifference I'm feeling: what I'm really feeling is resentment, but I'm feigning indifference. The BBC know exactly what they'll get if I make this film. They'll get my book *The Siege of Derry* boiled down to fifty minutes of factual television and making this pilot won't affect that outcome in the slightest. Yet they still demand we do it and that their meaningless commissioning process is faithfully adhered to. I'd like to think that the people who have devised this system (which is really a beauty contest) will end up in hell, and I am comforted by the fantasy of their eternity – a nook with dodgy strip lights, a duff computer and an infinity of Excel spreadsheets they can never get to balance.

eire

The Murder-Mystery Dinner (Saturday, 19 March 2011)

We are in the Rathmullan House Hotel, which is like a private house with big fires and old battered sofas and very lovely. In the morning we walked the beach and looked at a small Irish navy warship moored at Rathmullan, then spent hours in the pool and the steam room and then watched Ireland beat England (24–8, I think) at rugby. In the evening there was a murder-mystery dinner that we'd opted to attend. Our table, 'Taggart', had at it, besides us, a businesswoman and her husband (her name was Phil, short for Philomena; I didn't get the husband's name – indeed, he barely spoke) and a Belfast quartet of working-class Protestant women from the Beersbridge Road (mother Pat and daughters Florence, Leah and Michelle). At one point we were discussing naming children.

'When I was in my room in the clinic,' said Phil (she meant her room in the private Blackrock Clinic, having just given birth) 'and I was trying to decide on my daughter's name, I imagined her in a boardroom, introducing herself to the CEO as "Portia" and I thought, *Yes, Portia, that's a good strong name for someone in business.*'

Michelle beside me (short twenties-style flapper dress, a flower pinned to her front) followed with her own child-naming story. 'I didn't know what to call my daughter after she was born but I'd always loved Nicole ... And then after I got home from the RVH [a public NHS hospital in Belfast] and I still hadn't my mind made up, I remembered what someone, a friend, had said: "When you're naming her, just imagine standing at the kitchen door and calling her in to her tea – that's the way to decide if the name's right or wrong ..." and do you know, that's exactly what I did. I imagined standing at the kitchen door and calling, *Nicole, Nicole* ... and I knew straight away it was a lovely name, a perfect name, and that's the name I'd give her. And I never had a moment of regret.'

Well, there you have it, I thought, *the difference between North and South summed up*. A united Ireland is presumably, at some point, going to happen, but when I witness exchanges like the one I'd just seen, I do find myself wondering: how are these two bits, with their utterly different value systems, ever going to be joined together? And that sense that I had vis-à-vis the difficulties of making a unitary state got steadily worse as the evening wound on.

Somehow, we got onto a discussion about the history of our forebears and how complicated that history always is. I pointed out that all of us who were Irish sitting round the table (the only person who didn't qualify was my wife; everyone else was Irish and born on the island of Ireland) had ancestors who hadn't died in the Famine but had lived – hence we were having a conversation about them in the Rathmullan House Hotel 150 years later. And of course, I continued – a bit of a hobby horse of mine, this – to survive the Famine, what had they done? Who knew what they had done, but we couldn't be sure it was ethical or reasonable or right. People did what they did to survive and that was that, I continued, and then, as a means of accentuating the point, I told them my great-uncle by marriage had joined the RIC (pre-First World War, a good job for a Catholic) while his brother-in-law, my maternal great-uncle, joined the IRA. The policeman got accidentally shot by a fellow policeman and died of sepsis in 1921, while the IRA volunteer survived the War of Independence and the Civil War, only to die when a Mills bomb he was holding exploded prematurely in 1924. These men were on different sides, and what had happened in my family was mirrored throughout Ireland. Many families were split, some for and some against independence.

Phil, who'd voted Fianna Fáil in the last election (because that's what her father always voted), was having none of this. I should be ashamed of myself, she said, on account of my great-uncle by marriage 'flipping' (joining the police). She had no time for people like me and my kind, and we were not Irish, and we had no right to call ourselves Irish. And how did she arrive at this conclusion? she asked rhetorically. Answer: one was either for or against Ireland, and those who were for Ireland were the Famine sufferers (her group) and those who were against Ireland were the Famine profiteers (my group). In the Famine her group suffered (how did she know? She just did) whereas mine supported the British imperial project in Ireland, exported Irish food while the Irish starved, welcomed flippers (there was the word again) like my great-uncle by marriage (born forty years after the Famine but I said nothing about that), weren't Irish and weren't entitled to call themselves Irish. In fact – she really had the bit between her teeth now – seeing as we were a family of flippers (one policeman by marriage and we were all tarnished), we should all take ourselves off to England and never darken Erin's lovely shores again. That's what she said, despite the maternal great-uncle (my grandmother's brother) in the IRA. One further small point: not once during the meal did I mention my five children, reared and schooled on the island of Ireland, which indicates, surely, some level of attachment and commitment. That might have been a useful point to throw at Phil, but she would probably have suggested sending them to public school in England, as that would be the next best thing to the whole family moving away. On top of everything else, she was an incorrigible snob.

The old reactionary values of the Free State, despite all the window-dressing that suggests they are gone (better coffee, better roads, a professed admiration for the EU and the euro), are not gone. Indeed, they never went away. They just went down into the Irish collective unconsciousness and here they live and fester, and now and again, when the guard is down and the tongue has been loosened by alcohol, out they come, these absolutely abhorrent opinions: fascist, muddled and monstrous. *The job of the Irish writer,* I thought, when Phil concluded her magnificent peroration, *is to write about people like her and their values, pieties and prejudices.* We must make war on the morons and their beliefs, even though, as Jonathan Swift pointed out in his preface to *The Battle of the Books*, 'Satire is a sort of glass, wherein beholders do generally discover everybody's face but their own.' I would say it is absolutely certain Phil would never recognise herself in print, but so it goes and on we battle.

Three Encounters with Mr Bertie Ahern (Tuesday, 16 October 2012)

Sometime in the noughties I was in Charles de Gaulle airport. I went to my departure gate to wait for my afternoon flight to Dublin. I was early. I was very early. I am habitually early. But someone else was even earlier than I was, and I found him waiting in the horseshoe-shaped space when I arrived. Obviously, a passenger earlier than I was (and believe me, I was early) warranted scrutiny. So I stared. It was a man. Then I stared a tad more. I registered a broad forehead, small, shiny eyes, a pointed chin and then I thought, *Oh my goodness, could it be ...?*

And then there was that moment of hesitation I always get when I see someone famous in the flesh. This person didn't look like the man I had seen on television or in newspaper photographs. He looked a Xerox copy of the original, or even a fake. Then my brain's recognition software readjusted. And I knew. It was him. It was Ireland's Taoiseach, Bertie Ahern – medium height, solid build, relaxed, casual dress – standing at the top of the departure lounge near the gate facing the entrance.

He saw me see him as I entered and he saw me recognise him, I believe. What he did not see was what was going in my skull. One, I recognised him. Two, I thought, *The Taoiseach will definitely want to be left alone*. That's what I thought, and, determined to act on this, I sat down, got out my book – Alan Bennett's *Untold Stories* – and started reading.

A few minutes later the next-earliest (i.e., the third earliest: Bertie first, Carlo second, now herself) passenger arrived. It was a woman in her fifties. She clocked Bertie and without a second's hesitation flew to himself, grabbed his hand, shook it with an indelicate amount of force and began to speak, her accent pure Dublin.

'When I first saw you, I wasn't sure it was you,' she said. 'But then I realised it couldn't be anybody but you … It's funny the tricks the mind plays … and now, I am just so, so delighted to be shaking the hand of a living legend.'

The Taoiseach beamed. Being a bookish fellow, I immediately recognised the beam as pure Gatsby. His look told her, like Gatsby's told his guests at his legendary parties, that at that moment no one else existed in the world but her. And feeling the singular attention, which excluded everyone in the world but her, Colleen (by now I'd got her name) soared from joy to ecstasy. She'd had it all, she said, she'd seen it all … The great Bertie had shaken her hand in Charles de Gaulle airport and now she could die happy …

And what played out with Colleen was subsequently repeated by every passenger that followed – all right, not *every* passenger, but every Irish passenger who filed in after her. They all went up to their leader and introduced themselves, and he shook their hands and flashed his Gatsby smile at them, and they were delighted because here was the proof that the Irish and their Taoiseach had quite a different kind of relationship to the one other nations and their leaders had, for as this experience proved, the Irish and their leader were equals, citizens cut from the same cloth, who in a departure lounge in Charles de Gaulle airport of a Sunday afternoon mingled easily, happily, fraternally, democratically, rather than keeping warily apart.

The second time I saw Ahern was a few years later in a cavernous function room in a hotel in Ennis. The occasion was Síle de Valera's valedictory dinner when she retired as TD for East Clare. The guests were Fianna Fáil party members or those who had connections with the party and were prepared to pay for a plate. I was the guest of someone who had connections and had bought not a plate but a whole table's worth of plates. The Bertie I saw on this occasion was a different man to the one I'd seen in Charles de Gaulle airport. This wasn't man-of-the-people Bertie; this was Fianna-Fáil-are-the-greatest-party-and-don't-you-forget-it Bertie and, oh my goodness, what a force of nature was Fianna-Fáil-are-the-greatest-party-and-don't-you-forget-it Bertie. While the guests sat and ate, he spent the evening working the room; he talked to everybody, and I mean everybody. And there were hundreds of us.

And what he said to every person, he then repeated, with messianic gusto, when he got behind the microphone. There would be an election, he said; that's what this evening was about. Fianna Fáil would contest the election. And it was the duty of every single member of Fianna Fáil in that forthcoming election to give of their utmost in order to secure victory. They owed it to the party and, more importantly, they owed it to Ireland. Why? Because none of the other parties could be trusted to run the country. The party in charge after the next election had to be Fianna Fáil, and for that not to happen would be a disaster, not just for the party, but for Ireland because – and here was the clincher – Fianna Fáil were the natural party of government. They alone knew what Ireland needed, they alone could do and would do what needed to be done … and therefore it was everyone's duty to ensure that Fianna Fáil was the winner, et cetera, et cetera. It was quite a speech, absolutely devoid of vision, policy or truth, while also being powerful, persuasive and terrifying.

A few hours ago, I saw Mr Ahern for the third time … ah, the power of three. As I was passing the curious stub of lane connecting the Royal Irish Automobile Club to Dawson Street, I became aware, on my left side, of movement, of someone hurtling towards me along the stub. I started. They started too because of how I had started. The person looked up. I looked up. The person was a man. I registered the broad forehead, the small eyes, the pointed chin and once again, as at Charles de Gaulle airport, I went through the *Could it be? No, it isn't … oh yes, it is* malarkey. Only this wasn't the Bertie of yore. This was a very different Bertie to the Berties I'd met previously.

This was fallen Bertie. He was no longer Taoiseach (he resigned as Taoiseach 6 May 2008 in the wake of revelations made at the Mahon Tribunal). He was no longer leader of Fianna Fáil. He was no longer a TD. He was no longer even a member of Fianna Fáil; his party having proposed to expel all politicians censured by the Mahon Tribunal (the tribunal found Ahern, while not judged corrupt, had received money from developers, and the tribunal had disbelieved his explanation for those payments) he had resigned in March 2012.

This Bertie had lost the open, broad-faced, smiling expression of the Berties I'd met before and instead wore one that was weary and anxious. And this Bertie also saw me seeing him and a look of panic passed across his face. I wasn't surprised by his look of panic: since his fall, I imagined, he must have been endlessly accosted and berated by irate Hibernians furious with him on account of … well … take your pick: corruption, the 2008 catastrophe, the near collapse of the Irish banking system, the implosion of Ireland's economy, the bailout which obliged the Irish to pay the debts of others, the death of the Celtic Tiger. And now, here he was on Dawson Street, close to a fellow who had nearly collided with him and who clearly recognised him.

Was I another angry citizen? Did I look hostile? That's what I could tell he was trying to gauge. I wasn't, but judging by his reaction he judged I might be. Or alternatively, he decided he wasn't going to hang around and find out. He turned sharply, like on a sixpence, as they used to say, and sped away down Dawson Street in the direction of Trinity. Now, as it happened, I was going the same way and so I followed – not that I was following him, not technically, I was just going in that direction.

And as I went, my eyes went to the ex-Taoiseach and I noticed his coat. It was fawn coloured. It had a nice swing to it. I noticed his shoes too. Leather. Polished. Formidable. Impressive. And I noticed the shoulders. To my eyes they looked rounded, hunched, defensive. They were sagging, or so I felt, under a terrible weight. And the whole back, encased in the lovely coat, looked like the back of a troubled, harried man, and as I had that thought I remembered the passage in Eric Lomax's memoir *The Railway Man* about the pain that he, Lomax, felt when he had to stand with his back to those in the guardhouse in his Japanese POW camp who he knew were preparing to torture him. There are few worse agonies than the exposed back, says Lomax (who incidentally died a week or two ago), and I felt Mr Ahern's back similarly was prickling with anxiety – not just because of me but also on account of the whole Irish nation (or a large part of said nation) who had been glaring furiously, if metaphorically, at him for months. And as I sensed this (or projected this – it comes to the same thing), I felt something quite unexpected. He'd cocked things up mightily, yet I felt sorry for him, and I found myself wishing I'd set out a minute earlier or a minute later, in which case our paths wouldn't have crossed and I wouldn't have been a part of what he was feeling.

Dawson Street is long and I wasn't going as fast as Mr Ahern and he drew a good way ahead of me and then, as he approached within striking distance of Carluccio's, near the bottom of Dawson Street, his pace slackened. He peeled left, hand up in anticipation of pushing the door of Carluccio's open. I wondered what would happen next. Would he just go forward or, like Orpheus, would he just have to look? The answer, of course, was the second option. Mr Ahern couldn't stop himself, no more than Orpheus could. He glanced up to the street to see if I was there, and something crossed his face. I couldn't tell what – relief, outrage, despair, sorrow? Then he turned, shot through the doors and vanished from sight.

When I drew level with Carluccio's I glanced sideways. I too had to look. I saw the counter heaped with Italian patisserie. I smelt the coffee smell that always leaks out into the street through the doors. I saw a waitress, a dark apron. But there was no sign of the ex-Taoiseach. Perhaps he was already at a table telling someone he couldn't go anywhere in this damned town without being stared at, before scanning the menu and deciding what to order.

I walked on towards Trinity, and as I went I remembered Enoch Powell's famous dictum, which everyone always quotes because it is so memorable: 'All political lives, unless they are cut off in midstream at a happy juncture, end in failure, because that is the nature of politics and of human affairs.'

★

In November 2016, Fianna Fáil announced that it had given Ahern the option of rejoining the party. He rejoined in February 2023.

The *Revolutionary Road* Reader (Thursday, 1 August 2013)

At Dromod station I boarded the 10 a.m. train to Dublin. When I sat down I saw the woman sitting opposite me was reading *Revolutionary Road* by Richard Yates. A good book, I said. I am reading it for a special reason, she said. Her husband of twenty-two years, she said, had left her four weeks previously: he had no income, she added bitterly, so she'd not only lost her husband but she would also lose her house. Irish law, she explained. Because he had no income he would get half of the house. She was distraught, she continued, so distraught she'd taken off and put away her wedding ring because she didn't feel entitled to wear it any more, had taken up smoking with a vengeance and had lost a stone. She showed me the finger and pointed at the white band of skin where the sun had never shone when the ring was on. I was reminded of the walls of rooms when pictures are removed by decorators and the square pale patches where the paint hasn't aged that show up.

So why, I wondered, mired as she was in so much misery, was she reading *Revolutionary Road* – which has to be one of the most depressing accounts of marital catastrophe ever written? Because her mother-in-law, she said, had advised her to read weepies in order to get in touch with her feelings. I thought this suggestion perverse: it seemed somehow hostile. But I said nothing about that. Instead, I opted for the faux psychoanalytical tack. Did she really need to get in touch with her feelings? I asked. After all, wasn't she already very much in touch with her feelings? Didn't she already know she was miserable, inconsolable and bereft?

From my disinterested perspective, I – who was sitting on the other side of the table across from her – could see, all too clearly, that she was very much in touch with her feelings. Yes, all of the above, she said (a curious circumlocution), and she started to weep. It was tasteful and polite, unostentatious and demure weeping; obviously it wasn't done to sob in carriage B on the Sligo to Dublin Connolly train. What would the other passengers say?

However, it was obvious to me that this crying was the equivalent of a Potemkin village – that is, it was the kind which concealed a wretched truth: she was at the bottom of the pit and in utter despair. So what next? Where to go from here? Platitudes – 'Give it time', that kind of thing – they weren't going to work. She'd doubtless already had a bellyful of such encouragements.

But I did know a little bit about literature, and so for that reason I suggested she read *Love & Garbage* (Ivan Klíma). I said it was an uplifting book about love, which *Revolutionary Road* (despite its literary virtue) was not. (It is interesting that my idea of a charitable and helpful deed is not to suggest she read, say, P. G. Wodehouse – who many friends swear is guaranteed to raise anyone's spirits – but rather that she tried a different book about love to the one she was currently reading that is just a bit less depressing.) The *Revolutionary Road* reader liked this idea and said she would go to Hodges Figgis and buy the Klíma as soon as she got to Dublin.

Then she wondered if I'd ever considered dispensing book suggestions in a psychoanalytical sort of way. To help the heartbroken. The lonely. The abandoned. The marginal. Those maddened by suffering. That sort of thing. Book therapy, she said, with me the bookish therapist, or even the book therapist.

No, I hadn't, I said, but who was to say what the future would bring?

She liked this idea (it was her own idea, so she was bound to like it), and she said she thought I might have a glorious future awaiting me as the dispenser of bookish comfort. Then she stopped her decorous crying (though tears continued to flow and she had to dab them away from time to time) and for the rest of the journey we talked books and which ones might be proscribed for which ailment, which condition, et cetera, et cetera. She made a number of excellent suggestions. S. E. Hinton's *The Outsiders* for disgruntled teenagers, for example.

The train pulled into Connolly. Grey light, swooping pigeons. We alighted and she told me her name. We moved up the platform, talking as we walked. It was light and pleasant talk. I was engaged but simultaneously I stared about. Everyone around me in summer clothes. Sore patches of sunburnt white Irish skin. A child in jingling sandals, arms out, pretending to be a plane. A woman in a spangled cowboy hat and a jacket with rhinestones. At the end of the track, in front of the buffers, an oily puddle as black as tar. At the turnstiles, the magical ticket-slotting-barrier-opening thing, and we were through. Security men in paramilitary-black uniforms preening, Schwarzenegger-style, and glaring at the crowds. Out on the concourse, the smell of coffee and a sense of uptick and hope. Here about me were the citizenry of a country whose faces bore no resemblance to the old dismal ones I remembered. They were happier now, for though their country had plenty of problems (notably poverty and inequality: it was still an awful place to be poor and at the bottom), it had jettisoned many of the miseries that once oppressed it. It was a better, freer place and it showed. Here. On the faces.

Through the station's front doors, my companion and I went out. A knot of smokers on a bench. Young children sitting on the grubby floor playing cards. Onto the escalator. Slow descent. At the bottom, a man in a tracksuit on the pavement with a Styrofoam cup with change in the bottom, which he jingled hopefully. His face was a long Plantagenet face, a face you might see in stone outside a Norman church. It was a pale and desperate face. I'd seen this man here before. And I'd given money to him as well. My view is that it is better to be known as a giver, even an occasional one, than a skinflint; also, I've always believed you're more likely to get luck by giving than by withholding. (I have no evidence this is true, but I shan't let that stop me believing it is.)

I found a coin and dropped it in his cup. His eyes flicked up. Very dark, wary. A flicker of recognition. Yes. He remembered me. Or so I preferred to think. The woman and I moved along the rubbish-strewn Luas platform and stepped down onto the pavement. This was the end. I would be picking my way across the Luas tracks and heading left for Seán O'Casey Bridge and Trinity. She would be heading right, past Busáras and on to the city centre. We thanked one another for shortening the journey. I addressed her as 'the *Revolutionary Road* reader'. She addressed me as 'the dispenser of book therapy'. 'Hodges Figgis, here I come,' she said – she was going to try to find the Klíma, she repeated – and then she stepped away briskly and was gone.

'John [earthy Anglo-Saxon epithet for sexual intercourse] Bruton!' (Tuesday, 30 September 2014)

This being its centenary, the Government of Ireland Act of 1914 is being re-examined. With the outbreak of hostilities in the summer of 1914, the act, which would have given Ireland Home Rule, was suspended, the understanding being that once the war was over (and it was meant to be over by Christmas) it would be made statute, or whatever way laws are made, and Ireland would have Home bloody Rule at long bloody last.

But what is it they say about the best laid plans? The war didn't end by Christmas: it dragged on, interminably, and the Irish, or some of them, seeing England's difficulties offered Ireland (or them) an opportunity, staged the Easter Rising in 1916. The Brits overreacted; the Rising's leaders were executed; Ireland recoiled in disgust; in the elections that followed, the Home Rulers were defenestrated; Sinn Féin surged; the War of Independence followed; and ultimately, a very different Ireland to the one the Home Rulers had imagined came into being. In this Ireland they were the losers, and Sinn Féin and their tradition were the winners. But need it have been like that? (The devil's advocate question.)

Well, no, not according to John Bruton, sometime Fine Gael Taoiseach and a man, I think, who seems unable to resist putting his neck on any chopping block he passes. Mr Bruton has been arguing (a very touchy point this) that rather than having an uprising in 1916 (the Easter Rising) it might have been better to have waited for the Government of Ireland Act to have been enacted after the signing of the armistice, because this would have delivered an agreed Ireland – who knows, maybe even a thirty-two-county Ireland – and certainly not what we got, which was two Irelands (the Irish Free State and Northern Ireland) who were antagonists for decades thereafter (an antagonism which arguably lasted until the Anglo-Irish Agreement of 1985). Reaction to Mr Bruton's speculations has been predictably vituperative. Many have accused him of being a West Brit, insufficiently Irish, not a patriot, that sort of thing. Much vitriol has been thrown, or at least spilled in print.

The reason for the fury is not only that 1916 is a sacred event that lies at the pith of the nation's foundation myth, it's also just about the only event from our fraught recent past that isn't contested or besmirched or compromised: 1916 is the good one, the true one, the best one, our single perfect, unimpeachable moment, and we absolutely cannot afford for it to be sullied, questioned or picked apart by a blowhard opining that if it hadn't been done a better outcome would have resulted. Come on! How could there be a better outcome than the one we got? Cue outrage.

Of course, were we a mature society we wouldn't do it like this: a mature society would consider the proposition even if it disagreed with it. (It would also not let itself be affected by the fact that Mr Bruton has a knack of getting under the skin.) But we're not there yet. Far from it. We're still in medieval mode. Here, if a miscreant overthrows a shibboleth (our last shibboleth?), obloquy and abuse will be heaped on their head in the hope of drowning them out. And so, we howl, 'How dare he slag off the one good thing we've got, John [earthy Anglo-Saxon epithet for sexual intercourse] Bruton!'

Unknown Unknowns (Tuesday, 7 April 2015)

In the mid-1990s, thanks to Maurna Crozier, I started in the Maze. In 1997, thanks to my work in the Maze, I got a regular part-time job (bliss for a writer) as writer-in-residence at HMP Maghaberry: I owed this gift to Mike Moloney of the Prison Arts Foundation. He made the appointment. For years thereafter, prison was very good to me. Then, after nearly two decades I was – as modern HR people euphemistically like to put it – let go. By this time, both Maurna Crozier and Mike Moloney had died.

My final day as writer-in-residence in Maghaberry was Tuesday, 31 March 2015. The following Tuesday, the first in April, I felt slightly at sixes and sevens, and was unable to settle, this being the first Tuesday in a very long time when I hadn't had to go to the prison to work. My wife was also not at work as she usually would have been, and she suggested we treat ourselves to a day in Belfast at the Ulster Museum.

We set off. My wife drove. The engine thrummed, the hot air from the dashboard blowers wafted into my face, trees and fields, hedgerows and villages flashed past. I fell into a lightly tranced state, and instead of directing my thoughts, my mind was in receiving mode and the thoughts came, one after another, like fireworks in a night sky come one after another, with each detonation a thought that was wild and bright, brilliant and extraordinary. As we passed Lough Neagh (a vast pool of molten solder lying flat in the distance), there came a flurry of thoughts related to work and my future ... My prison job was finished, I thought, so I had no need to stay in Northern Ireland. I could return to London. That might be lovely. Or maybe I could be more adventurous. I could move to Italy, perhaps, and learn Italian ... or go to the south of France and learn French. It would be a new beginning, a new life. Yes, why not ... Everything was swirling and dreamy when the biggest firework yet whizzed in and exploded, lighting the sky gold and carrying a thought as categorical as it was absolute. I couldn't go away. No. Maurna Crozier and Mike Moloney, who'd done so much for me, had died here, so here I must stay. In Ireland. On this small damp island. I owed it to their spirits, because that's what the living did. They stayed where the dead were.

When this fantastical idea arrived, it seemed perfectly plausible for a moment. Then the rocket expired and the sky went black again. The thought was so unexpected and spectacular I was shaken from my tranced state and restored to myself. Wow. Had I really thought what I'd thought? Yes, I had. I began to wonder about its origins. I presumed it was an inheritance, from my prehistoric ancestors, which normally would have lain undisturbed, down in the unconscious. Only today my mind wasn't functioning as it typically functioned. It wasn't in charge, and so ancient and archaic material could get out for once.

In the Ulster Museum my wife and I went to look at and were hugely impressed by *The Four Seasons*, the gigantic mural the Enniskillen painter William Scott made for the entrance to Altnagelvin Hospital in Derry. (The work was a commission: Altnagelvin was the first new National Health Service hospital built in the UK after the end of World War II, and presumably a bit of aesthetic pizzazz was wanted, seeing as this hospital was the start of a new progressive era, health care for all, free at the point of delivery, et cetera, et cetera.)

The Four Seasons was painted on four huge wooden panels and was completely abstract yet completely concrete – I knew as I looked which panel belonged to which season – or so I would like to think. So how did I know? Not by relying on my reason, anyway. The meaning was encoded in some non-rational way in Scott's markings, and it was only thanks to some non-rational capacity in my psyche that I understood what was what, that was for sure.

In the museum we were also hugely impressed by Con O'Neill's Chinese porcelain collection (oh my Lord, the dishes – so pure, so simple and so perfect) and the Henry Fuseli exhibition. This consisted of eight or ten pen-and-ink drawings of female adults: according to the catalogue, the women featured were all either prostitutes or Sophia, Fuseli's wife. Every figure had incredible hair. The draughtsmanship was extraordinary (never has hair been rendered with such exactitude or exaggeration); but there was also something else going on in the drawings, something disturbing. One example: a head, female, from behind, with hair that was an amazing sculptural confection of plaits and curls, braids and bobbles, swags and strands. There was a second figure in the background, again, with incredible hair, but it was only after a while that I realised this second figure, who only wore a gauze shift – or was it a shroud? – was naked, and when I twigged this, which initially I hadn't because the rendering of the hair of the first figure was so overwhelming and so engrossing, it was a real shock. In drawing after drawing Fuseli pulls off the same trick. He gets you looking here, so you miss what's over there.

When I got home I started Rob Doyle's novel *Here Are the Young Men*. It's about four young working-class Dublin blokes. They take a lot of drugs and drink a lot; they are swaggering, dysfunctional, emotionally illiterate and totally unable to relate to girlfriends, to women, to females, to the feminine. *Oh crikey*, I kept thinking as I read, *what has gone wrong with men* (of whom I am one)? *Why are they* (we, me?) *the way they* (we, me?) *are?* Doyle doesn't offer an explanation but he tells a truth.

Besides being disturbed (and appalled), I was also uplifted by what I read and I sensed (and the sense was certain, unequivocal) that I will be reading this writer in ten years, in twenty years. This chimed with the day's theme for me, which was all about not seeing and seeing, not knowing and knowing: some things I can't see because they're submerged and I need the right circumstances – inattentiveness, say – in order to see them; some things I won't see (Scott's *The Four Seasons*) using my surface, rational faculties and I have to use another faculty, hidden deep in the psyche, to see them; some things I can't see (the shrouded woman's body), even though they're staring me in the face, because my attention is elsewhere; and some things I see, or think I see (a writer's future, for instance), based on – well, something in myself that can do this future-seeing thing, but over which I have absolutely no control.

The Brexiteer (Thursday, 24 March 2016)

The Crumlin Road Gaol was a nineteenth-century construction, built to replace the clink in Carrickfergus. It was decommissioned as a working jail on 31 March 1996 and is now a tourist attraction; however, tucked at its rear and still functioning is the working-out unit – this is where long-term prisoners, coming to the end of their sentence, spend the last few months before their release and are prepared for liberty. As an aid to the process, the artist Anne Scullin and I are running a programme of museum visits, theatre trips, excursions and conversations for men from the unit to help them prepare for life beyond the prison gate. And they need it. They've been in prison so long their capacity to function is shredded …

It was late afternoon when I left the schoolhouse for the jail. The sky was inky. I drove eastwards through Augher, Clogher and Fivemiletown and then along the motorway. I drove on automatic pilot until I saw the giant steel globe where the motorway ends on the edge of Belfast. Here I turned the automatic pilot off, for now I needed to concentrate. I skirted the roundabout anticlockwise, and when I emerged on the other side I got a good view of the Westlink ahead, jammed with rush-hour traffic. I knew it would be a long haul to the Crumlin Road, and it was, and as I crawled along I listened to the radio: BBC Radio 4, *PM* and the *Six O'Clock News*. Brexit featured heavily, David Cameron having announced on 20 February that there would be a referendum which will offer the United Kingdom's population the choice of whether to remain in or to leave the European Union … The BBC's coverage didn't strike me as impartial. The EU being a bad idea appears to be a given.

Finally, finally, nearly there. On my left the wreck of the Crumlin Road Courthouse (it had been set on fire by arsonists); on my right the old Crumlin Road Gaol. A little further on I turned in to a lane and drove to the steel gate at the end. I stopped and waited for the camera to clock me. Once it had, the gate juddered back. I slipped through and found myself in a yard. The working-out unit looked like a factory on a light industrial estate. An officer waved at me cheerily. He was not in uniform. Uniforms are not mandatory here and the regime is relaxed; prisoners go out to work or to education every weekday and have overnight paroles at weekends.

I parked and went into the unit. Inside, I found myself in a large room with a pool table. Prisoners just returned from work or parole were being breathalysed or debriefed by prison officers in the pod at the rear. Other prisoners were sitting around or cooking in the kitchen. The atmosphere was nothing like the atmosphere on a prison wing at this time. It was muted, subdued. Everyone here knew that shortly they would have to give up everything with which they had grown familiar over the ten, fifteen, twenty, even twenty-five years they'd been in prison and return to a world utterly unlike the one they'd left. They all yearned to be released, but at the same time they were all terrified and anxious of what awaited them on the far side of the gate. Would they make it? Maybe they wouldn't, and they all knew men who'd left, failed dismally outside and been returned to prison.

My programme tonight was simply to talk. And the man I was going to talk to was George, someone whom I already knew. His life was one long misery fest. Working-class parents: his father went to work; his mother stayed at home. Not much money and absolutely no comfort or cheer. No drinking, no pleasure, no fun. A cold, joyless house and church (twice) on Sunday. The politics of the home were unionist. This family were staunch. Sectarianism was present if casual. He hated school; book-learning didn't suit. His parents' antagonism to education and teachers reinforced his own loathing of education. As early as possible he left school and got a job. He hoped a wage would impress the family, especially his father, who was emotionally unavailable. It didn't impress. They just took his money.

He grew a bit resentful. A bit rebellious. He drifted into drinking and soft drugs. The family, especially the father, were appalled but, as he saw it, he was entitled to fun and the old folks could fuck off. The fun led him to loyalism: he became a small cog in a Protestant paramilitary organisation. He did nothing of much significance – painted some kerbstones on the estate before the Twelfth, held a gun overnight, hid some ammo, that sort of thing. It didn't amount to much but it did wonders for his confidence. One or two scraps, then, with republicans. Got a bit of a reputation. Hard nut. Always good to have if you met the Taigs. Boy, did he stick it to the fuckers. The years ticked by ... a bit of drinking, a bit of drugging, a bit of fighting ... twenty, twenty-one, twenty-two ...

He was living at home, feuding with his parents about his habits and his lifestyle. He realised he needed to do something, get a steady better-paying job than the one he was doing, get a girlfriend, marry that girlfriend, settle down, buy a small house, have a family. He joined the UDR (Ulster Defence Regiment) as a part-timer. He absolutely loved it. There was the uniform, the gun, the camaraderie, the money and the many opportunities being in the army afforded to stick it to the Taigs. And he was still in touch with his old loyalist paramilitary contacts. He passed on little titbits of info and they were very pleased, very, very pleased, and they said the nicest things to him about what he was doing. He was, they said, a good man, staunch, a real patriot who was standing up for Ulster.

Life was looking up and things just got better and better. He had money in his pocket. He found a woman. He married the woman. They bought a little house. They had some children. He had his job in a warehouse and his part-time soldiering and she had a part-time job and life was good. But he was still the needy boy. His parents were alive and despite his successes he longed for their approbation, especially his father's. He still drank, actually he drank rather a lot, actually he was an alcoholic, if truth be told, and he took as many drugs as he could get and miraculously avoided getting caught and cashiered from the regiment. The marriage now began to suffer. He and the missus drifted. He suspected infidelity. He began to watch her. But he was very careful. Gave nothing away. Gave her no reason to be anxious, gave her no sign he knew something was afoot.

One evening, thundering rain. He was out on patrol but he wasn't far from home and he was very wet, and he wangled permission from the officer in charge of the checkpoint; he could nip home and change into some dry clothes. He ran through the drenched streets in his sodden uniform and let himself into the marital home. He was not expected – nor was he heard, so loud was the rain.

He found his wife in the lounge. She wore nothing. She was with a man. She ran. Her visitor ran. She ran rearwards, into the garden. The lover ran forwards, out the front door and away down the street. The husband ran after his wife. He had his gun, his personal protection weapon, but he didn't draw it. He grabbed a pair of garden shears that he used for clipping the hedge (they were in the kitchen; he'd been sharpening them) and followed her into the garden. She was trying to scale the fence, the wood slippery with wet. He pulled her back and threw her onto the sodden grass and stabbed her to death. His children were upstairs in their bedroom, which was at the back and overlooked the garden. At his trial he claimed he was out of his mind but the judge declined this plea for mitigation. George was sentenced to life and given a hefty tariff. The state appealed, seeking an increase. The judges ruled that if George had shot his wife in the lounge, he might have been able to plead provocation; but he hadn't shot her there: he had found his shears and followed her outside; his actions were to a degree premeditated; they upped his sentence by four years.

The conviction and the sentence broke him: his family disowned him; his children were taken by his wife's people and he knew, once that happened, he would never see them. His early years in jail were dire; he was full of self-pity but not remorse. But then something happened internally, as is often the case. He began to think he'd better do something; he began to think he'd better take advantage of what was on offer, and what was on offer was education. He did GCSEs and A levels and eventually an OU degree in sociology. This changed him. He became more open-minded and more curious and much more politically enlightened.

He also become interested in prisoners' rights. In the UK, as he had discovered, prisoners endured a kind of civil death because after sentencing they lost the right to vote. He believed it was quite wrong prisoners didn't vote. I was in complete agreement and this is what I started talking to him about, with particular reference to the EU's recent attempts to get the UK to allow certain categories of prisoners to vote in elections for the European Parliament. We talked about why the British government was resisting and whether or not the right to vote in European Parliamentary elections, if achieved, might one day lead to prisoners in the UK being able to vote in

Westminster elections. George thought yes, possibly, that could be the case, but that narrow good shouldn't sway us in regard to the much bigger matter now in play: the referendum. No, sir, he certainly wasn't going to let prisoners' voting rights possibly being advanced by the EU stop him voting Leave.

'You want to leave? Why?'

'It's in the national interest.'

'Excuse me?'

'If we don't get out, we soon won't have a country, will we?'

'We won't have a country?'

'Yeah, we're being overrun.' Here he used a succession of nasty words for Eastern Europeans. 'They're taking over,' he said.

'They're taking over?'

'Yeah, and the way things are going, we're soon going to be a minority in our own country and no one will speak English any more.'

I decided to ignore this and focus on the benefits. I argued that the EU was a body which, though bureaucratic and slow-moving, had improved things in the UK. But he wasn't having any of that. If the EU was so good why wasn't the nation flourishing? It was obvious: the EU was to blame, holding the country back. But if the UK left (thus escaping the tentacles of perfidious Brussels – he actually used this phrase) the future would be glorious.

I knew a little about George's private life. A few years earlier he'd asked a prisoner who was leaving prison having served his sentence to find him a pen pal. Female. The prisoner found a woman who was prepared to correspond. Letters were exchanged. The woman visited George in prison. On his first parole they met up. One thing led to another. They became an item. And they were still an item. And when George was out on paroles he stayed with her and he slept in her bed. This generous, loving soul had taken him into her life and heart, even though he was a life-sentence prisoner; she had even suggested that perhaps with her mediation and intervention it might be possible for George to get back in touch with his children when he was fully released. She was also an EU national, Black and Catholic. Maybe it would do no harm to remind him of what might happen to the woman he loved.

'What about your partner?' I said. 'What's going to happen if Leave win? Will she be able to stay? And what about this tiny little additional awkward fact: if we hadn't been in the EU, she wouldn't have been able to come and live here; and if she hadn't come to live here, you wouldn't have met her; and if you hadn't met her, think what your life would be like.'

He didn't like this much. He waved his hands and shook his head.

'Don't you worry,' he said, 'the UK is very big-hearted. She'll be fine.'

'Really? How do you know that? What evidence do you have?'

A long wrangle followed but he wouldn't give ground. What I had to understand, he said over and over again, which as an Irishman it would be difficult for me to grasp (ouch), seeing as how my country (Ireland) had taken so much money from the EU (ouch, ouch), was that the UK needed to take back control and stand on her own two feet. And the UK would be fine doing her own thing. He was sure of it. Once the UK stopped being bossed around by people in Brussels, she'd become a great country again. And the other reason to leave, he repeated over and over again, were the immigrants. Because of freedom of movement they were flooding in, driving down wages, taking all the houses, clogging up the schools, gumming up the hospitals, et cetera, et cetera, but when the UK left that flood would stop, and when that happened wages would rise, rents would fall, class sizes would shrink, crime rates would collapse and hospital waiting times would vanish.

I tried a different tack. 'Are you really telling me,' I said, 'Boris Johnson and Nigel Farage and Arron Banks and Tim Martin and

Michael Gove and all the others working for the Leave campaign are individuals you trust and that you can honestly say, hand on heart, "Yes, I believe they're good people, sincere, honest and trustworthy, and that if they get their way and win, the UK will be a better, fairer, happier, nicer country." Do you really believe these individuals are big-hearted, because they look anything but big-hearted to me?'

No, he said, I was quite wrong. They were good people. Generous, wise, compassionate. I had nothing to fear. He was sure of it.

The rush hour was over by the time I left, and the Westlink was empty. So was the motorway. I didn't listen to the radio as I drove. I felt too depressed to listen because now I knew exactly how the vote in the June referendum would go. The Georges of the country, with their nonsensical ideas about racial purity and the greatness of the UK once she was unshackled from perfidious Brussels, would edge it. Leave would win. I knew it.

An Ashen Donald Tusk, a Smirking Tim Barrow (Thursday, 30 March 2017)

Yesterday, staged for the cameras, European Council President Donald Tusk received by hand from the British ambassador to the EU, Tim Barrow (a man with the face and beard of a Victorian patriarch), Theresa May's letter to the European Union triggering Article 50, which will initiate the UK's exit from the EU. The photograph of the event on the cover of today's *Guardian* showed Tusk looking pained, even ashen, while Barrow looked to be smirking. I wondered if he was embarrassed by what he had to do (hence the smirk) or, alternatively, if he relished his part in this upending of the apple cart. Was he keenly looking forward to the time when old Brexiteers would gather round him in the saloon bar and beg him to tell them about the day he stuck it to the EU? Tusk's interview, given following the dismal handover, broadcast last night and reported on today, was notable for the upset he showed. He was emotional. Really troubled. Sad. It showed in his face, voice and posture.

His public display of grief – he clearly does not want the UK to leave the EU – reminded me of the iconic photograph of Mrs Thatcher with tears in her eyes sitting in the back of a ministerial car as she sped away from 10 Downing Street after she was toppled by the Tory party. She had feelings. Of course. Failure and discord and rupture cause pain, and pain is felt.

And other EU officials who were quoted echoed Tusk's grief. The EU and its personnel really do not want the UK to go. In Britain, this is neither acknowledged nor understood. In the right-wing press, all that yesterday's events produced were acres of crowing: at long last we've finally done it; we've stuck it to the foreigners and the Brussels junta; why, oh why, did it take us so bloody long? In the *Guardian*, on the other hand, the focus is on what will happen to the UK; the *Guardian* and other progressive commentators are disturbed and perturbed by the future they see looming (falling trade, isolation, loss of prestige, loss of European connections, a general slide into mediocrity and mendacity and irrelevance). But understanding the misery of our European allies was not really addressed, although the *Guardian*, to be fair, did acknowledge it was a 'thing', even if they didn't dwell on it. The question that interests me is why do the British, and particularly the Tory Brexiteer clique, have no empathetic faculty at all in this regard? I have two answers.

- Perhaps the lack of insight is rooted in a fear of being found out. The EU human response is not the response of a tyrant but the response of a genuinely hurt and aggrieved party. However, as the EU has been characterised as a tyrant (like the Nazis, like the Soviets, take your pick), its human response, its grief, can't be acknowledged because that would undermine the we-are-throwing-off-the-shackles-of-oppression narrative.
- Or perhaps the lack of insight is simply because they – the Brexiteers – are so drunk on hubris, so intoxicated with their own rhetoric, all they can express is their vicious joy, the conviction they are right, their uncritical certainty. There's no room left for the other in their inflated, narcissistic, self-centred world. They're the victors, and victors have no need to show compassion to the vanquished, the defeated.

But whatever is the explanation, this lack of insight is a terrible failing, a national failing, a failure of state craft. As even the densest of our masters must know, in real life, if you are leaving a spouse who does not want to lose you, no one bar a blockhead would demonstrate the lack of insight and empathy that the English (British) are showing the EU. You'd know it is dangerous and it will create enmity. You wouldn't crow. But our masters have crowed and gloated and this bodes ill for the future. If you behave truculently with a hurt and spurned partner, especially when you separate from them, they will treat you truculently in turn when their chance comes. And their chance will come. We live beside them. We're going to have to work with them. The portcullis might be down and the drawbridge might be up for a few years, but it can't stay like that for ever. And then what, when we realise we need them? It won't be pretty. We really are in for a rough time because of our triumphalism.

On *Drivetime*, the RTÉ Radio 1 evening news programme, the Brexit discussion contained the assertion that as far as Ireland is concerned, Britain (or the UK) was their big brother and they hate to lose him. After centuries of misery and turbulence (Ireland's experience of Britain was catastrophic, and in Europe the only parallel would be Poland and what that nation had done to them by Russia and others) this is now the Irish view of the UK: it sees the UK as a big brother. This is extraordinary and also rather wonderful.

So why would you want to jettison that? It must be madness, surely, to discard the good will that has accumulated despite the awful past. And why is there no sense in the UK that this is Ireland's opinion? If it was known it would perhaps give even the most hardened Brexiteers a slight shock. It might make them stop and think. We've got a land border between Northern Ireland and Ireland, which will become the land border between the UK and the EU: we'd better be careful with that ... But all these things that show Brexit is really not good but actually bad, and which might encourage reflection and generosity by the UK, aren't being communicated. You certainly don't get any sense of these contrary opinions, and the necessity of moving gently and not wilfully destroying a relationship that has been so carefully constructed, from the BBC or from the majority of the British press. Yes, living in the UK at the moment is almost like living in a one-party state where only the party's opinions are promulgated.

A Prisoner (Saturday, 29 December 2018)

In Hydebank (a prison outside Belfast for women and youngish men) a prisoner came up to me in the education room. He was in his twenties, wore terrible prison-issue clothes (a grey tracksuit, slightly yellow around the crotch where a past wearer had soiled himself) and had a bright gleam in his eyes; it was like the gleam in the eye of the Ancient Mariner who waylays the bridegroom, I thought. He was drinking a ferociously strong cup of prison-issue coffee, and because of the way he cradled his cup I could see his wrists were bound in bandages (slightly grubby): he had recently cut himself. I knew this prisoner, had known him for years. He was currently in for a long list of thefts and public-order offences and had been in prison many times for the same sort of offences. He had no home and when at liberty he slept rough in Belfast. Many of my fellow teachers have seen him in Belfast, been accosted by him in Belfast, and one or two had even given him money.

'You think I'm stupid,' he began. 'Everybody thinks I'm stupid. I'm not stupid but I want them ... you ... to think I'm stupid ... that way you'll underestimate me and that's the way I like it. I don't want you knowing or understanding what's going on in here, in my bonce.

'My mother had different kids to these different men, and my father, I never knew him, and then, when I was three, we all came here from Scotland and I grew up in Cookstown and then my stepdad died when I was twelve and we were wild and we were taken into care and I fucking hated it. So one day my friends are coming to the home to get me and this fellow who works for the home, a member of staff, he makes me look like a stupid cunt, a complete stupid cunt, in front of me friends and I think, *Right, you're not going to make a cunt of me* ... So I goes into the kitchen and I gets a knife and runs back and I stab the cunt in the kidneys and then all the staff run into the office and lock themselves in and I think, *Right, Donal, here's your chance.*

'I get petrol and I lay a line from the fuel and gas tank at the back to the hall and then I light the trail and the flame goes bang and one of the tanks goes bang and the hall goes up and they have to send two fire engines and it's fucking fantastic and the police come of course and I'm charged and all that but they let me stay and I'm thinking, thinking, thinking, thinking, *You made a cunt of me, you made me look stupid in front of my friends, well I'm going to teach you a fucking lesson.* So I break up all the furniture in the hall and I set that on fire one day and, well, then I'm out, I'm double charged and now no hostel will take me cos I've got arson, twice, on my charge sheet and that's why I've been living on the streets for four years.

'I don't want to be good. I hate good. I hate peace too. I want to earn my living by doing criminal things. That's what I am, a criminal, and so that's what I want to be, a fucking criminal, doing fucking criminal things, earning his living doing crime. That's what I am. I know what I am. And don't talk to me about change. I don't want to change. I want to be left alone. I want to be what I fucking am. And don't talk to me about being a goody two-shoes neither. Fucking boring being good. No, no, don't be good. Be bad. That's the way to live. That's the way to have an exciting life. Being a goody two-shoes is a waste of time. A waste of time. I know, cos I'm not a goody two-shoes and I have a fantastic fucking time, a fantastic fucking time, and all you goody two-shoes, your lives are dead and boring.

'It's chaos in here in my head and I fucking want to see chaos outside in the world to match the chaos in my head. Don't talk to me about peace. I fucking hate the word peace. I hate peace. I hate this talk of peace. I hate the word. Give me chaos. If I had my way it would be chaos all around. Anyone wanted, I'd give them a Kalashnikov. They can go and make chaos then. I thrive on chaos, of course. That's why I need it. That's why I want it. Bring it on, I say, all the wars in Iraq and Syria and everywhere else. Happy days.

'I'd only change if I had a wean and it would have to be some fucking woman who'd make me change. Obviously, I'd try to find a woman who took drugs but then supposing she didn't, well, then I'd think about that, I'm not saying I would, but I'd think about it, I'd think about settling down and that, maybe.'

As soon as the morning's session finished, I went to my car in the car park, fished my phone from the glove box and dictated from memory as much of Donal's fantastical spiel as I could remember.

★

About a year later, coming up to Christmas, I was in Belfast. Twinkling lights, the smell of mulled wine, festive merrymakers in Santa hats and reindeer horns. I was skirting the back of City Hall when I saw Donal with another man sitting on a sheet of cardboard in a dark doorway. I approached. I smelt skunk but whether Donal had been smoking I'd no idea. He was holding a grubby Starbucks cup with coins in the bottom, like pebbles in a stream.

I greeted Donal. He heard me. He lifted his head slowly and looked at me. I don't know if he saw me or knew me. I hunkered down, took out my wallet and pulled money out and offered what I'd plucked out. It was ten pounds. Donal looked at the note very carefully and for a long time. His companion was looking at the note as well. He elbowed Donal. 'Donal,' he said, as if to say, Don't let it go. Don't let it slip through your fingers. This is a tenner, mate! *'Donal!'*

Eventually Donal took the note very gently. He folded it carefully and slipped it inside his glove. His companion hadn't taken his eyes off me and I now heard his dog, who I'd only just noticed, a grey whippet, whining quietly. Everything about this moment was subdued and thoughtful, and I had the uncanny feeling that I was not in time but out of it, somewhere else, another dimension.

'Do you know who I am?' I said to Donal. 'Do you remember me?'

Donal looked at me very carefully.

'How do you know him?' said the other man.

'We met in another life,' I said. I assumed the other man must know Donal had been in prison but I didn't want to say it.

'Oh,' he said. 'In jail.'

So much for my tact, *I thought.*

Donal was still staring at me, his eyes very dark and still. 'I'm going to die out here,' he said.

Donal's companion didn't like such talk. 'Come on,' he said. 'You'll be all right.'

'No, I won't,' said Donal. 'I'm fucked.' He nodded at me. 'I'm fucked, aren't I, boss? I'm totally fucked.'

POST OFFICE
Collection times
12.45pm

There Is Absolutely Nothing to Recommend about the Ageing Process (Thursday, 3 October 2019)

I was born in 1954. So this year I turned sixty-five and embarked on my sixty-sixth year on earth.

Now, given the year what's in it, the British state, which previously only ever communicated either to ask for money, or to tell me I was in trouble, has been bombarding me with bits of paper connected to this calendrical milestone. First there was the letter from social security in Newcastle, from where pensions in the UK are organised.

Dear Karl, the letter began (for I am known to our friends in the north by my baptismal moniker), your pension will be coming, only not when you expected, i.e., now you've got to sixty-five. Owing to a shortage of funds, it's being postponed a bit.

I was, I must say, not in the least bit miffed to receive this. In fact, I was actually quite pleased. If the pension were deferred then that meant OAP-hood was deferred too, didn't it? Yes, I thought so. Technically, I might be sixty-five and pensionable, but really, I wasn't. Or so I kept telling myself.

Next there was the communiqué from the Belfast health board containing the bowel cancer self-tester kit. Emulating Mrs Beeton's recipe for jugged hare ('First catch your hare …'), the instructions began,

'First catch your stool …' Once caught, the instructions continued, I was to use a wooden spatula (a fistful were provided) to dab some stool into a pair of recessed cardboard reservoirs. I was then to repeat this procedure over successive days, dating each entry of course (this was a fiendishly complicated process), and once the task was complete, I was to send everything back to them in the special leakproof SAE they'd thoughtfully provided. If it turned out something was wrong, my GP would be in touch. Otherwise *nada*. That's what the letter said.

I did as I was told but heard nothing from the GP and, I have to say, I wasn't just pleased about that, I was elated. Not hearing meant 'it' hadn't happened, and seeing as 'it' only happened to the old, this meant I wasn't old *yet*.

Then came the letter about my first-ever flu jab, which I was offered of course because of having attained the big six-five, and on receipt of which I found myself obliged to perform a very complicated psychological fandango. Your health, said the professional hypochondriac inside me, is good and, in the normal run of things, you shouldn't need to have this flu-jab thingamajig. However, Mr Hypochondriac continued, seeing as you're back into the prisons, working, and seeing as the wings are rotten with germs, you should do this to protect yourself, but that's nothing to do with the age thing …

Impeccable logic from himself, I thought, and with a lightly fluttering heart I made an appointment for my jab. It would be on a Thursday afternoon in early October.

The Thursday came. Today. I entered the health centre where my GP's practice is based: I was a working man, still in his prime …

Inside, humming neon lights, a warren of rooms and corridors, the sick lounging about (*Crikey, I hate the sick*, I thought, sauntering past them: as a hypochondriac, of course, anyone whose germs might breach my defences is persona non grata), the special surgery smell (disinfectant wipes, witch hazel, liquid nitrogen) and counters with receptionists (all inscrutable unreadability and Sphinxish hauteur) who also seem unchanged since childhood.

I found my GP's reception desk and, as I had been instructed, said I was there for the jab. Then I added that I'd sit and wait in the usual waiting area.

'No, sorry,' said the receptionist, 'but would you mind *not* sitting in the general waiting area.'

'Not the general waiting area?'

'No.'

'Where the magazines are?'

'No.'

'Somewhere else?'

'Yes.'

'Where there are no magazines?'

'Yes,' she said. 'It's a temporary arrangement.'

But I was looking forward to leafing through ancient copies of the *Ulster Tatler*, a publication I only ever see at the doctor's. I particularly like the pictures – which are always to be found in the *Tatler* – of the province's bourgeoisie in their best frocks and tuxedos at Marie Curie fundraisers and Rotarian dinners. I like these photographs because they allow me to sneer at the bourgeoisie, and nothing puts snap in my celery like a good sneer at the bourgeoisie; and seeing as that's what the bourgeoisie were invented for, I am determined to have my sneer time. I will not be denied my sneer time. It's really the only thing I enjoy when I come to see the doctor (everything else about the doctor is hideous). And if I understood correctly, I was now being denied this pleasure? Holy moly.

'Really! No mags?' I said.

'No,' she said.

My eyebrows rose. The receptionist waved at the corner behind me. 'Please go and sit over there and Hermione will collect you when she's ready.'

Hermione will collect me? What, like a parcel?

I didn't actually say that. I just said, 'Hermione will collect me?'

'Yes, Karl, Hermione will do that when she's ready. So take a seat, Karl. Hermione will be along presently.'

People with authority, I've noticed, typically revert to the exclusive use of forenames in only two circumstances: either when you're an infant or when you're an oldie, which was what, seemingly, as far as this receptionist was concerned, I was. Really? *Hermione will collect me.*

The receptionist returned to the keyboard and I turned to see where I was supposed to go. OMG. It was the corner by the double doors that led to the toilet – i.e., in health-centre terms, it was Siberia; and it was packed with old people, all of whom, to my jaundiced eye, looked like dry, wrinkled prunes. And I was supposed to sit with them, in public? Of course, I didn't want to. I didn't want to be bracketed with the old; I wanted to be bracketed with the young, even though I was there as an OAP to have my shots. The one thing I am certainly consistent on is not being consistent. But of course, it's what keeps me young.

The receptionist, sensing I hadn't moved, looked up and did something with her hand. It was a quick flicking gesture. It said, *Go on, off you go, away with you* … So to those with whom I did not believe I belonged, I must go. Well, needs must … I would be graceful … Nothing became him like his departing, blah, blah.

I sidled over to Siberia and settled into a seat in the middle of the OAP corral, then raised my *Guardian* high to screen my face. If I wasn't seen then it followed I wasn't part of this crew. Yes, I know, magical thinking, but it's always worked for me.

The minutes ticked by, then Hermione's door flung open and there she was, sprightliness incarnate.

'Malcolm,' she said.

Malcolm crept into Hermione's surgery and a few minutes later crept back out again and came up to us.

'Didn't cry, so I didn't,' Malcolm announced for our collective benefit. I couldn't help noticing he'd gone in with his jacket buttons done up right but come out with his jacket buttons comically misaligned.

'Brave boy, aren't I?' Malcolm continued.

I didn't laugh. Nobody did. Something had to be said about the buttons, though, so I said it.

'Buttons,' I said.

Malcolm dropped his head and saw his front buttons were in the wrong buttonholes.

'Oh,' Malcolm said.

Malcolm began to undo the first button. His hands were shaking so much that in the time it took him to get the first button back out through its slit, I could easily have written a haiku. Or two.

Stop with the fucking buttons! I wanted to shout, but instead I ventured, 'Shall I help?'

'No,' Malcolm said calmly. 'I prefer to do it myself.'

I prefer to do it myself. Holy hell.

Hermione was at her door again, and this time it was a trio who responded to her summons, two ancient parents plus their almost-but-not-quite-as-ancient son. Terrifying. A whole nest of oldies.

The trio shuffled off and in, and we who were left watched as Malcolm, with painful difficulty, undid two more jacket buttons. Then he did them all up again and of course – of course – when he did them up again, they were still all bloody wrong. I didn't say anything. Nobody said anything. What would have been the point? We'd all have just had to sit and watch as he did the same thing again. It would have been like watching Tantalus in Hades failing to get his drink over and over again.

Eventually, my name was called. I went in to the surgery and sat down opposite Hermione.

'You're here for the wee flu jab?'

'Yes.'

'And would you like an extra wee jab for the pneumonia and the meningitis?'

If the use of wee once was bad, its double use was intolerable. *Why are the jabs wee?* I wanted to ask. *Do you think I'm a frightened wee child?* I said nothing, of course. I just smiled and said, 'I'll have both. Thank you, that would be lovely.' My irony went unnoticed.

A minute later, having been pricked twice (and, no, it didn't hurt – it was just two wee jabs), I emerged from Hermione's lair.

One of the waiting old, just outside the door, was a pale-faced fellow in a hideous tomato-red windcheater, the colour of which definitely did not match his pallor.

'Anything strange to report?' he asked me.

I knew immediately what he was up to. He was trying to bind me closer into the group; he was trying to make out I was one of them, and he wanted me to know I was, and he wanted me to agree I was, but I was having none of it.

'No, nothing strange to report,' I said and fled. Nobody was getting me in this club. Not as long as I was breathing.

Sunday at Florence Court (Sunday, 8 March 2020)

The morning news reported infections and deaths in Italy from coronavirus are so high that the authorities have introduced a lockdown in the north of the country, starting this morning, to contain the spread of the disease; the news also reported the biggest overnight jump yet in the number of cases in the UK. This means that at some point in the not-too-very-distant future, we will have to do what the Italians are having to do now. We will all have to go into our houses, bolt the doors, shutter the windows and stay there until the plague passes and we are told it's safe to come out.

In the light of what will happen, my wife and I decided to have a last hurrah, a day out. Florence Court House is a National Trust property (with grounds) in the foothills of Cuilcagh Mountain. It is the seat of the Earls of Enniskillen, who are the descendants of the ur-planter, Captain Cole, a Devonian appointed by James I to build an English settlement at Enniskillen and hold it for the Crown and England. The captain did as tasked: he prospered mightily, as is so often the way when conquest is followed by colonisation (what a brilliant economic model that is for the victors), and he established the line that built the lovely house and laid out the lovely grounds at lovely Florence Court, which was to be our destination.

We packed the car with coats and umbrellas (it's always necessary to bring everything in this climate where you have all kinds of weather *all the time* rather than one kind of weather at a time) and set off. When we got to Florence Court we learnt this was Discover Fermanagh Open Weekend and the usual charges didn't apply. Ecstasy ensued, and as my system flooded with endorphins or whatever it is that gives pleasure, I remembered an article I'd read about the joy we experience when we're let off paying what we habitually have to pay for; this kind of joy is seemingly much greater than the joy we feel when we get a gift, say, even a gift we've long coveted. I presume this explains why politicians are keener on tax cuts than handouts; they calculate (correctly) the pleasure of being let off having to pay tax is more likely to secure votes in an election than pressies ever will. As it's traditionally right-wingers who put tax cuts at the centre of their campaigns, are we to conclude they're better psychologists than the parties of the left?

The day was a mix of rain and sun. We tramped through the woods (woody, mushroomy leaf-mould odours, wet shining grasses, shimmering fern fronds with stiff curled edges) and then the formal gardens (rhododendrons with pulpy leaves, flinty gravel paths shining with damp, children in wellingtons splashing in gleaming puddles). Then to the tea room (where else do you go after a National Trust trudge?), which is a cavernous, churchy space that feels cellar-like though it's actually ground floor; all the tables had little jugs with fresh flowers and miniature glass milk bottles for milk (how National Trust) and the walls were hung with lovely black-and-white domestic family photographs taken by someone in the Cole household and dating from the era of the fifth countess, Irene Frances Miller Mundy (date of birth unknown; she died 1937). No one knows who took these photographs. Not for sure. It may have been the fifth countess, though there's no evidence it was (oh, how quickly the details of the past perish). I think there is a good chance it might have been her who took them, though, seeing as the pics are mostly of her children: sitting astride ponies, the bridles held by ancient Irish grooms; swimming in cold Irish water on a sunless, chilly day in their old-fashioned combinations; walking in the gardens on an Sunday afternoon with their father, the fifth earl, John Henry Michael Cole (1876–1963), dressed in their Sunday best and looking a bit frightened … and so on.

These photographs are incredibly evocative of the social life of the Cole family in Florence Court in the 1930s. However, alongside what they say about the collective, they have an existential meaning (or to me they do, at any rate). The Coles and their Anglo-Irish class, say the photographs (and this knowledge belongs to the photographer, whoever that is, as well as the subjects of the photographs), know their power and prestige is shrinking. For a start, the British, their patrons, have just, ten or fifteen years earlier, been unceremoniously ejected from four-fifths of the island of Ireland (an astonishing achievement when you remember the asymmetry of the adversaries in terms of power; really, how did the Irish pull this off?). And even though the Coles are lucky – they haven't been left behind in the Free State: they're in Northern Ireland, with its Protestant Parliament for a Protestant People, which will always side with people like them – for their caste, the establishment of the Free State represents a defeat. Then, on top of that, there are their mounting economic problems. Their capital is shrinking, which will ultimately force the fifth earl to give Florence Court to the National Trust in 1963. The Coles had their time in the sun, back in the eighteenth century, but those times are long over and now the clouds are massing.

We went to the servery to get tea. There were only a few people ahead of us in the queue. It was a much smaller crowd than usual. (Clearly the virus was already causing people, or at least the middle-class people like ourselves who are National Trust members, to stay at home.) As I took my place at the rear, I noticed I didn't stand quite as close to the next person as I otherwise might. From watching the news and reading the *Guardian*, I had acquired the bewildering and brand-new idea – which, for the first time in my life, I was now acting upon that somebody else, like the nice lady in the beret, standing just a few feet in front of me, might, just might (it was statistically unlikely at this moment but it was not impossible), if I got too close, give me something that would make me sick, so sick I might, if unlucky, even die. Interestingly, the reverse was not on my mind. I did not think I might be carrying it, and I might give it to her in the beret. No, my only thoughts were about the danger posed by other people to me, rather than by me to them. Clearly, self-interest is baked into my psyche; this is something I've known since forever yet, amazingly, I keep rediscovering this truth over and over again.

After tea, we took a peek at the newly restored kitchen garden and then we came back and did the 4.10 p.m. house tour (it was also free – more joy). I'd done the tour before but what I heard this time was new to me. The fourth countess, Charlotte Marion Baird, from Dumfriesshire (b. 1851/2), a redhead (how did that go down? I wondered; red hair was – and sometimes still is – associated with Irish ethnicity and Catholicism), lived in the house for many years and built the garden and bore her husband, Lowry Egerton Cole, fourth Earl of Enniskillen, nine children; then, in 1910, she got back part of her dowry, left Ireland (and her husband, the fourth earl, who died in 1924) and went to live in Florence (like a Henry James heroine). She was still in Italy when she died in 1937. Though the excellent tour guide offered no explanation for Charlotte's decamping, I thought as I listened that the story of the chatelaine who leaves her Irish mansion, reclaims some of her dowry and goes abroad might be one worth telling in fiction. (I am always on the lookout for material that might be transmuted into copy.)

But within seconds of having this thought came the realisation that what I was next hearing might be even better as the basis for a work of fiction. Irene Frances Miller Mundy of Derbyshire, whose photographs I hoped I'd seen on the walls of the tea room, had married the fifth earl, John Henry Michael Cole, on 11 April 1907 (thus becoming Charlotte's daughter-in-law). The couple had four children; then, in 1933, the guide explained, Irene left Florence Court and vanished. Nobody knew either why she left or where she went; she was just gone, and for three years nobody knew where she was. Then, in 1936, Irene got back in touch with her children, but the guide wasn't able to say if she ever saw them. The guide did think Irene divorced her husband (he subsequently married Mary Cicely Nevill), though she didn't know when this happened. After hearing this, I began asking questions. Was there really nothing known about why Irene vanished? And was there not even an inkling as to where she was for the three lost years and what she was doing? No, the guide repeated, it was a mystery. All she could offer was that Irene's marriage wasn't a dynastic match: it was a love match; only then something happened, nobody knew what that was, and the marriage foundered.

As the tour continued there were further unknowns: these concerned the house and its origins. It is not known, we were told, exactly when it was built, nor who designed it (although there are various candidates, including the German architect Richard Cassels, who built other Irish houses). Nor was it known who lived on the land before the house was built. But somebody was there, though their names had been forgotten or deliberately erased. The plantation of Ireland is littered with such lacunae. The plantation is an event that happened, and we have the proof that it happened in the form of the estates, which still exist all over Ireland and which we trek reverently around, admiring the furnishings, enjoying the paintings, savouring the views, but what exactly happened, the nitty-gritty as land was expropriated from one group and passed to another group, coercively, is all too often vague or unknown. This was certainly the case in Florence Court House. And suffering for sure was involved. How could it not be? Fermanagh wasn't empty when the first Cole arrived. It had an existing culture which he, and other planters, supplanted. So I found myself wondering as I wandered on through the house, can you be made miserable by your sense of what your ancestors and predecessors have done to others in the past? Did the generations of the Cole family who lived in Florence Court through the eighteenth, nineteenth and twentieth centuries feel oppressed by a sense of the hurt their forerunners had inflicted when they dispossessed the Irish, before they built the lovely house in which they were living? Does trauma linger? And could somebody like the fourth countess, or better still, the fifth countess, even though she was not a Cole but had married in, have sensed this and been oppressed by it? And could that have been a factor in her disappearance? Questions, questions, but so often in Ireland that's all you really have, because so much of the past, the past being a time when so much was contested, has vanished. L. P. Hartley famously has it at the start of *The Go-Between* (a favourite book) that 'The past is a foreign country: they do things differently there', but in Ireland the past isn't a somewhere else, different and alien; in Ireland the past is an absence, a void, a hole, as is so often the case with those places that have been colonised.

★

After writing this entry up I did a bit of research. I couldn't find anything out about the private life of the fourth earl and his wife but I did turn up a very public event which couldn't have been helpful to their relationship. Charlotte married Cole in 1869. A year later, her new husband was cited as one of two co-respondents in the case for divorce brought by Sir Charles Mordaunt, tenth baronet, former MP, against his wife, Harriet, in which Prince Albert Edward, the Prince of Wales (later King Edward VII), was called to give evidence. The divorce was denied as Lady Mordaunt was judged to be insane; however, it was finally granted in 1875, and this time Cole did not contest the claim that he was the father of Lady Mordaunt's daughter, Violet (1869–1928), later Marchioness of Bath. So the year 1869 was not only the year Charlotte married Lowry Egerton Cole; it was also the year Lady Mordaunt gave birth to his daughter Violet. Did Charlotte discover this the year she married? Or did she find out courtesy of the first divorce proceedings a year later? Or did she not know until the second proceedings in 1875? With her husband not contesting he was Violet's father, it would have been a miracle if Charlotte hadn't got wind of what had happened by this point. But despite looking, I could get no fix on when Charlotte knew and what exactly she knew. I couldn't even confirm she did know.

Charlotte died on 30 January 1937, pre-deceasing her daughter-in-law Irene, who died on 15 August 1937, by nine months. Had they ever corresponded after they both fled Florence Court? After all, it is quite something for the wives of the fourth and the fifth earl to flee the same place.

Nature abhors a vacuum but writers love them, for they offer a space to fill. I turned this story over in my mind for a bit after my Sunday in Florence Court and I decided the place to start, if I was to make something of the story of Charlotte and Irene, was Charlotte's house in Florence. It's 1933 … it's morning, and Irene, who has recently left Florence Court without telling anyone and travelled by train across Europe, appears at Charlotte's front door, harried, frayed, exhausted, carrying nothing but her camera, and explains, having fled Ireland, and the family, and the house Charlotte herself fled twenty-three years earlier, she has come seeking sanctuary and begs her octogenarian mother-in-law to take her in …

ULSTER
~~1912.~~
2021?
TIME TO
DECIDE!

The Northern Ireland Centenary (Monday, 3 May–Wednesday, 5 May 2021)

Hyper-vigilance is our default setting in Northern Ireland. When you have our history, you pay close attention to every new mural, every new poster, every newly painted kerbstone. It's the only way to anticipate what's coming. So when a neighbour raises a flag overnight, you don't ignore it.

We're not in the schoolhouse at the moment; we're staying somewhere else while a new floor goes down. We're in a cottage in an Irish wood outside a village a few miles away from the schoolhouse. In the morning, when I woke up in the cottage, I got up and went to the window and I pulled the curtains, and that was when I saw that my neighbours across the road had run an orange flag up their flagpole. Every year the Orange Order celebrates the victory of William III of Orange, who defeated the Catholic James II at the Battle of the Boyne in 1690, so I assumed it was for that that the flag had been run up. Except no, I realised, that was wrong. The Battle of the Boyne was in July, and July was two months away and Battle of the Boyne flags would never go up this early.

After breakfast, my wife and I put on our coats, mine a worn Barbour with shiny patches where the waterproofing has worn off, hers a stylish Max Mara Weekend off-white puffa, and set off on our morning walk.

We schlepped down the frosty road and stopped to look at the flag I'd seen earlier. I saw it bore the legend '1921–2021 Northern Ireland Centennial Flag'. Mystery solved. Ah yes, today (which I had vaguely taken on board and then promptly forgotten – after all, why would one want to remember the centenary of a country that has never really worked and, it has to be faced, probably never will) was the hundredth anniversary of the foundation of Northern Ireland. So that was why this flag was flying.

We tramped through the local village and came to a stop at the main road to Belfast. SUVs lumbered by, and while waiting for them to pass, I noticed something stuck to the nearby Give Way sign which hadn't been there when I'd passed on my morning walk the day before. It was a reproduction of a UVF poster repurposed for 2021.

The original had circulated in Ireland in 1912. Back then, it had seemed that Home Rule would deliver a parliament in Dublin with an inbuilt Catholic majority; this would have robbed Protestants, unionists and loyalists – most of whom were concentrated in Ulster – of their British identity and connection. So the answer to Rome Rule was to stand and fight, like the woman in the shawl clutching a rifle with the union flag fluttering behind. Now, in 2021, Irish domination was back, along with the loss of British identity and connection for Protestants, unionists and loyalists. Only this time, it wasn't Home Rule that was the problem but the Northern Ireland Protocol, agreed to by the UK because of its departure from the European Union.

In order to avoid a hard border on the island of Ireland, in January the UK established a de facto trade border down the Irish Sea, and some see this as a calamity that will ultimately culminate in a united Ireland. Earlier this year there were several nights of rioting in Derry and Belfast. The participants, none of whom, I think it would be fair to say, would ever accept being in a united Ireland, rioted in order to make clear their antagonism toward the protocol (which, by separating them from Britain, will edge Northern Ireland closer to unification with the south), along with a number of other grievances: these included the way republicans breached Covid restrictions at the funeral last summer of IRA stalwart Bobby Storey, as well as a general perception that the Protestant, unionist and loyalist community has lost ground everywhere, while the other side, the side represented by Sinn Féin, has gained ground everywhere. For some in Northern Ireland, the zero-sum game is still the default; as the rioters saw it, they've lost, the other side has won, and the only way that can be fixed is for them to win and the other side to lose. The poster on the Give Way sign was calculated to reinforce such thinking: 1912 was scored out; 2021 was the new date when doughty Protestants, deserted by Britain, would stand and fight alone.

We crossed the main road and followed the old one to Dublin, admiring a gnarled milestone marooned amid bungalows and black asphalt – the words 'Enniskillen' and 'Dublin' barely legible on its crumbling face – along with a lovely Church of Ireland church surrounded by clipped lawns and tidy graves. Then we passed into the countryside of Fermanagh, rumpled like a bedspread, with low brown hills in the distance. Now and then cars went by, and as they did every driver slowed and gestured. Those gestures were no more than a finger raised from the steering wheel, but the freightage of neighbourliness was unmistakable. Yes, within half a mile of the poster with its incendiary message, civility abounded. But that's Northern Ireland; everything is jammed together cheek by jowl, good and bad.

We turned in to a trelliswork of smaller roads edged with spiny hedgerows full of wildflowers (the names of many of which my wife sang out) and behind which stretched a patchwork of small fields, many rank with rushes, until we came to an ancient Irish churchyard, perched on a hill and surrounded by a high stone wall. Inside were half a dozen ragged Irish yew trees, a broken-down chapel and a lumpy expanse of tottering tombstones and broken crypts. As we wandered around reading the inscriptions, one in particular caught my eye: 'Here lies the body of Redmond McManus who died in 1744 aged 76 years old ...'

A quick calculation (when you have to do the mental arithmetic, you actually can) suggested that Redmond McManus was twenty-two in 1690 when William triumphed at the Boyne. The battle's impact on Redmond would have been huge, but whether it was good or bad would have depended on which side he was on. From his name, I guessed he was on the losing side, the Irish side, the Catholic side. Of course, he might have converted, which perhaps would account for his long life.

Thus, I ruminated, as one so often does living here. Our history is a sore tooth and the tongue keeps darting to it. How can it not? Our past isn't some faraway concept, full of bad things people have agreed not to argue about. On the contrary, our past is still a wound: thus Catholics, mostly, do not celebrate the Boyne. We like to say we did away with sides and history when the Good Friday Agreement was approved in the 1998 referendum, but as the repurposed anti-Home Rule poster told me, that's not true. Some of us are extremely committed to our side. At the moment, because of the protocol, it's largely the Protestant side that features in the news, but the other side hasn't gone away. During the spring riots, the worst violence was when the so-called peace line was breached and youths from the two sides, republican and loyalist, clashed. For the moment, rioters of both varieties are a minority, but what is the future? I don't know the answer, but what I can say is that I'm reading the runes: the flags, the posters, the murals, the kerbstones, the statements from politicians, the newspaper articles, the things I hear people saying

– people I know and people I meet casually – and I am trying to work out what they mean.

We left the churchyard through a creaking metal gate, descended the hill, and walked on to the last station on our walk: a tiny, beautifully proportioned, cut-stone Georgian gate lodge that stands abandoned at the side of the road. We admired it and then, as we made our way home, we fantasised about buying it, doing it up, coming to it on Sundays to have tea and maybe sleeping in it overnight. Yes, even as the runes seem to murmur ominously, we dream … about doing up properties.

Over the last academic year, I have accumulated a mound of essays written for me by students whom I teach at Trinity College in Dublin. Owing to coronavirus restrictions, I couldn't take them to college for shredding, so I arranged instead to burn them in a furnace on a farm, and on the Wednesday afternoon, two days after that Monday-morning-Centenary-of-Northern-Ireland-walk, filled still with thoughts (and premonitions) provoked by the repurposed 1912 UVF poster I'd seen, I drove to the farm with the furnace and, as I turned in to the yard, I spotted Martin cleaning a ditch. I know Martin well. He has mowed my lawn, cleared my gutters, unblocked my drains and brought me firewood. I lifted my finger from the steering wheel as I drove in, and he waved in reply.

In an outbuilding, I consigned the essays to the flames while starlings flittered overhead, and when I returned to my car I found Martin waiting to talk. We spoke of the weather, our health and our kith and kin, and then he told me – this was his big news – that his brother had taken thirty acres. The land, he explained, belonged to a man who couldn't farm it and so, for as long as their agreement ran, it would be his brother's land. Here, his brother could put out his cattle or sheep, or cut the grass for hay or silage, which he could then sell on or use to feed his own stock. This being such a novel development in his brother's life, Martin had just been to walk the fields, on Monday, the centenary of Northern Ireland's founding, in the morning, as it happened; so I'd been tramping the lanes when he'd been up the mountain tramping the brother's fields.

'What's your brother paying?' I asked. 'Is he getting a good rate?'

Martin looked at me and shook his head, delight on his face. 'Oh no,' he said. 'The brother has the fields for free.'

'For free?'

'As long as he tops the rushes and maintains the hedges and the gates, they're his for nothing.'

I'd never heard of anything like this before. Astounded, I pressed him: had the brother really got these fields for nothing?

Yes, he had, Martin assured me, and then he became positively loquacious. The fields, I should understand, were up the mountain. It was wild and lonely up there, as everyone had left. All the houses were empty. And with no one left to do the farm work up there, his brother was doing the owner a favour. The arrangements were interesting, but not as interesting to me as the abandoned dwellings Martin had mentioned.

'Are all the houses empty up there?' I asked.

'Yes, they're all empty.'

I mentioned the gate lodge my wife and I had admired and asked if there was anything like it up the mountain.

'To be sure,' said Martin.

'Which way would I go if I wanted to find your brother's fields?' I asked. 'And see these houses?'

Martin named a local town. I was to go to the corner where Vernon Crowther was murdered and turn there. In Northern Ireland it is not uncommon for places to be identified by a violent or catastrophic incident. It could be something from the distant past, but equally it could be something that occurred during the Troubles. This particular incident had taken place then, when the IRA had attacked and killed two members of the RUC – one of whom was Vernon Crowther –when he and a colleague were on duty and out and about in a car.

'Do you know the corner I mean?' Martin asked.

Of course, I did. In a place like this, you know these things. Our landscape is shaped by such places.

'And did you know him?' Martin asked.

'Not personally, only by name.'

'Nice fellow,' said Martin. 'Vernon's farm was beside our farm. He and my father did no end of business. In and out of our house every day of the week, so he was. One time he was there and I had this old gun and I said, "Vernon, I can't hit a thing with it!" He took the gun and, quick as you'd blink, didn't he drop a crow? "Nothing wrong with this gun," he said, handing it back. "It's you that's wrong, young Martin." Being a policeman, he knew his way around guns, and I didn't; that's what he meant.'

Martin then proceeded through the murdered policeman's entire dynasty, reeling off who had died when, and of what, until he came back to Vernon, shot dead in a car at the corner where I was to turn for the road to the mountain.

'I didn't go to his funeral,' Martin continued. 'You know … on account of my religion. I didn't want to cause botheration.'

A woodpecker started in a tree behind. The noise was uncanny. Martin put his hands in his pockets. He'd told me something important and now he wanted the weight of what he'd said to settle in. Funerals matter in Ireland, which was why the Bobby Storey incident was so incendiary. But Martin hadn't attended Vernon's funeral because he was anxious that if he, a Catholic, went to the funeral of a Protestant policeman murdered by the IRA, the other mourners might have taken offence or got upset. They might have assumed, because he was a Catholic, that he supported the IRA. They might even have thought he was there to record the car registration numbers of the other mourners, many of them also policemen, with the intention of passing these details on to the IRA so they could murder them too.

After he judged enough time had passed for me to grasp the import of what he was saying, Martin started up again. 'I did want to go,' he said, 'and I should have gone, but I couldn't. Do you understand?'

Oh, I did. But as I stood there with the woodpecker hammering behind, I wondered what a third party eavesdropping on us would make of our conversation and Martin's disquiet. First, there was that odd segue from directions to tumbledown houses to funeral protocol if you're a Catholic and the deceased is a policeman. I didn't find that turn in the conversation the least bit odd. I'd experienced such turns from the ordinary to the extraordinary before. But how would someone who hadn't find this turn? Wouldn't they find it odd? And then there was Martin's confession. It had been his duty, he had implied, to attend his neighbour's funeral. But he had violated his sacred obligation in the hope of being tactful, and it troubled him still because his decision was seemingly also wrong.

I said goodbye to Martin and drove to the schoolhouse, intending to work. It had been sunny but now the clouds had darkened. From the door of my study (the old bicycle shed, separate from the house) I surveyed the sky and thought about Martin's attempt at tact and, because it was so singularly without tact, the repurposed 1912 poster. To the naysayers who would do away with the protocol, like the maker of that poster, Martin is on 'the other side'. His Catholic confession codes him Irish and maybe a supporter of a united Ireland; his funeral story suggests he's more complicated than the label allows, but this kind of complexity tends to get discounted or ignored in this culture; one is as one's badged and this is why our ancient rancours and the divisions they insist upon are still as alive in 2021 as they were in 1912. We're all in our tribes – well, some of us are. Fortunately, though, our ancient capacity for charity – practised by both traditions – is also still intact, which is what I tell people when they ask why I live here.

A few moments later, it began to hail, the stones coming down hard and heavy. I abandoned thought and gave myself up to the pleasure of watching the green fields turn totally white. The Irish flag – a divisive symbol – has three panels: green for one side, orange for the other and a white panel between the two, the symbol of peace. In my imagined future, the Irish flag would have no panels. It would be all white. White is my favourite colour. Most people think I'm a lunatic for thinking things like this, but frankly, I don't give a damn.

★

On 24 March 2023 the British government and the European Union concluded the ludicrously named Windsor Agreement, which supposedly has made the border in the Irish Sea almost go away. Sadly, despite the agreement, the signage (anti-EU, anti-protocol, anti-Windsor Framework) hasn't.

TAMLAGHT
WILL
NEVER
ACCEPT A
BORDER
IN THE
IRISH SEA!
50

An Accident Followed by an Invasion (Thursday, 24 February–Friday, 25 February 2022)

On the train from Dublin Connolly to Dromod last night, I caught the news on the iPhone. It was wretched: Russian troops were massing in Russia and Belarus … President Vladimir Putin was talking tough … 'Ukraine, the puppet state of the EU and NATO, is run by neo-fascists … The state is a mediocrity, an excrescence that needs to be wiped out, squashed like a louse …' My reaction was a queasy mix of sympathy (how awful for the Ukrainians) and relief (what a mercy to be so far from where something terrible was about to begin).

I got out at Dromod station – a cruel wind blowing, not a night to be out – and jumped into my car. I cued up the *Magic Mountain* audiobook and nosed from the car park, Thomas Mann's crystalline prose filling the car's interior. In Dromod village ghostlike mist patches floated along the pavements, but there was not a soul in sight. Out in the country beyond, a Bible-black night (to borrow from Dylan Thomas): no moon, no stars. In the next village, Mohill, no customers were vaping outside the pubs like they usually are; I saw only two pedestrians, both carrying takeaway pizzas in plate-sized greasy boxes. On the other side of Mohill, back in the country again, the houses and small farms and bungalows I passed were silent and subdued. Fenagh was utterly deserted and the pubs were dark. Ballinamore was the same. Beyond, in the country again, gaunt hedgerows and bare-limbed trees unfolding beside me, I thought of charcoal drawings on rolls of paper that went on forever. Meantime, the text of *The Magic Mountain* was playing; the chapter was the incomparable 'Snow': Hans Castorp loses his way in a snowstorm, falls asleep, his sleep as near to death as it is possible for sleep to be, and has extraordinary dreams. I was absorbed by what I heard, but I was also aware that out on the edge of my thoughts small fires of anxiety were flaring up. The world, the world.

Nearing Swanlinbar, I started along a stretch of road that twists and turns across a worked-out bog that is much lower than the road itself. Knowing there is a precipitous drop on either side (if I were to slip off here, I'd be done for), I slowed, and as I slowed I saw the hazard lights of cars ahead, one facing me, one pointing the other way, my way. I saw people too, but they were wispy, nebulous, hard to make out. I turned off *The Magic Mountain*, wound down my window and passed the first parked car; the monotonous sound of the blinking hazard lights drifted in. I drew level with the figures. There were four. They were all peering into the ditch. Someone had what I assumed was a mobile with the torch function on and was holding the phone over the ditch, pointing the light down.

'Has there been an accident?' I called.

There had. A cyclist had gone into the ditch. He had been pulled out. His bicycle too. But he had lost his glasses. In the ditch. They were trying to find them. I had a torch, I said. A big one with a nine-volt battery. Would they like me to join them? I asked. They said they would.

I parked and got out. I got a better sense of who was who now. Two of the party were brothers, I assumed. They had the same rheumy eyes and ancient tortoise faces. Then there was the cyclist, thin and wiry, gashed badly across the face. His yellow high-vis jacket (which I couldn't help noticing was tied with orange bailer twine) was sheeted with thick, viscous blood. The fourth figure was in her early twenties and wore a black fitted dress with sequins, which glittered faintly in the gloom. She had a broad, wide face with much make-up on it, curly hair and enormous earrings. She looked like a performer, I thought, about to step on stage. The mobile phone being used as a torch was hers.

I turned on my torch and pointed its beam down. I had just put in a new battery so the light was good. The sides of the ditch were covered with thick, long grass. The grass was very wet, so wet that every blade was bent by the weight of the water attached to it. *Fronds underwater in a Jacques Cousteau film*, I thought. In the bottom of the ditch, which was a long way down, brown water ran. The bicyclist was talking. He couldn't do anything without his glasses.

'I'm blind without them,' he said, sounding distraught, and then he spat out the blood that had got in to his mouth while he'd been speaking.

'We'll find them,' said the woman. From the way she spoke I knew she knew the bicyclist and he knew her.

We searched on together, the five of us, moving now one way and now the other along the verge, and below us the long grasses swayed hypnotically and the water at the bottom of the ditch ran brown and cold. Once someone asked were we looking in the right place and someone else said it had to be, just turn around and look, and so we all turned and we saw the bicycle on the other side of the road, propped against a black telegraph pole, its front wheel buckled, its handlebars twisted. This was the spot; around here, surely, somewhere, the lost glasses must be lying. We searched for a long time but we didn't find the spectacles and eventually a halt was called.

The bicyclist produced his own mobile. He had to ring home, he said. The trouble was, he couldn't see the keypad. He held the phone out to the woman. If he called out the numbers would she dial? She said she would.

Both bent over the phone and their faces were lit from below, hers serene and lovely, his bloody and fraught. He called the first number out. Her finger, the nail varnished bright red, went toward the number, but before she could get to it, a great glob of his blood plopped down and covered the screen. The bicyclist wiped the phone's face on his jacket, but that simply smeared the blood about and made things even worse.

'Come on,' she said. 'This is no good. I'll drive you back.'

'My bike ...?' he said.

'We'll come back for it in the morning,' she said.

They turned and began to walk towards her car, her heels clicking on the frozen road as they went. I turned towards my own car ... and that was when I heard her shout, 'Here they are.'

I turned back and saw – she angled her phone so they were illuminated by its white, pale light – his spectacles, arms out, lenses glistening, lying in the middle of the road (so perfectly arranged, they looked as if they'd been placed there by a film props person). I had driven right over them, I realised, and miraculously I hadn't flattened them.

I slept badly that night, and I woke before dawn, edgy and a bit fretful. The light leaking through the schoolhouse windows had the peculiar tinny lustre that it only has if snow has fallen. I got up and went to the window and saw that our drive and the lane and Thompson's field all the way to the gorse hedge at the top were carpeted with what looked like hard, slightly creamy-coloured icing, for snow had indeed fallen during the night. It wasn't falling now, but from the light I knew there was more to come, much more, and I knew it was going to snow all day.

I got back into bed. The sheets were warm. My wife murmured. I turned on the radio and heard the Ukrainian media was reporting that the Russian army had crossed the border and entered the country.

No. one. Cares.

Suffocations, Old and New (Friday, 27 January 2023)

As a child, I suffered from asthma. In adolescence, it stopped and I hardly thought about it for decades. Then, following the Tory victory under Boris Johnson in the 2019 election, memories of the asthma years began to surface.

Initially I thought this must be to do with the ageing process. I am now in my seventh decade, so it seems perfectly plausible that my childhood brush with mortality would loom larger and larger as I drew closer to the end.

But that hypothesis then gave way to another, neater one. It was my pattern-loving brain doing its pattern-loving thing. In childhood it was particulates, in adulthood it is politics, but both, I was being reminded, make me feel as if I'm suffocating, which is true.

Ruminating further, however, I found myself feeling disappointed. (Seemingly, I'm never satisfied.) Is that it? I wondered. Was that the wisdom of the unconscious? Because if it was, that seemed rather insufficient. And pedestrian too. No, there had to be another, better reason for the asthma reveries. So what was it?

For a while I got no answer. And then this morning, it came. It wasn't the suffocating then and the suffocating now that was the point. It was the story of the asthma that was the point. When I was young I'd had asthma; then one day it stopped. And the same will happen in politics. One day Johnson will go, the Tories will go. And then it will be possible to breathe again.

★

Once I could vote, I only voted Labour. In the EEC referendum I voted in support of membership. Once I moved to Northern Ireland, as I couldn't vote Labour (they didn't organise here), I voted for the Ulster Unionists in the Westminster elections (under the first-past-the-post system there was no point voting for Alliance or the SDLP in the Westminster constituency of Fermanagh and South Tyrone) and for the Alliance Party, the SDLP, the Ulster Unionists, the Greens and the occasional socialists who stood in the local government and Stormont elections, which used the single-transferable-vote system as opposed to first-past-the-post system. In the 2016 referendum I voted to remain in the European Union.

Following the UK's exit from the EU, I determined that if unification with the Republic was the only way back into full membership of the European Union, well, that was fine by me. I no longer believed in any other future but that one, or in the United Kingdom for that matter. The IRA failed to move me with their campaign of violence to overt support for a united Ireland but good old Brexit has. Ah, Brexit … the gift that goes on giving.

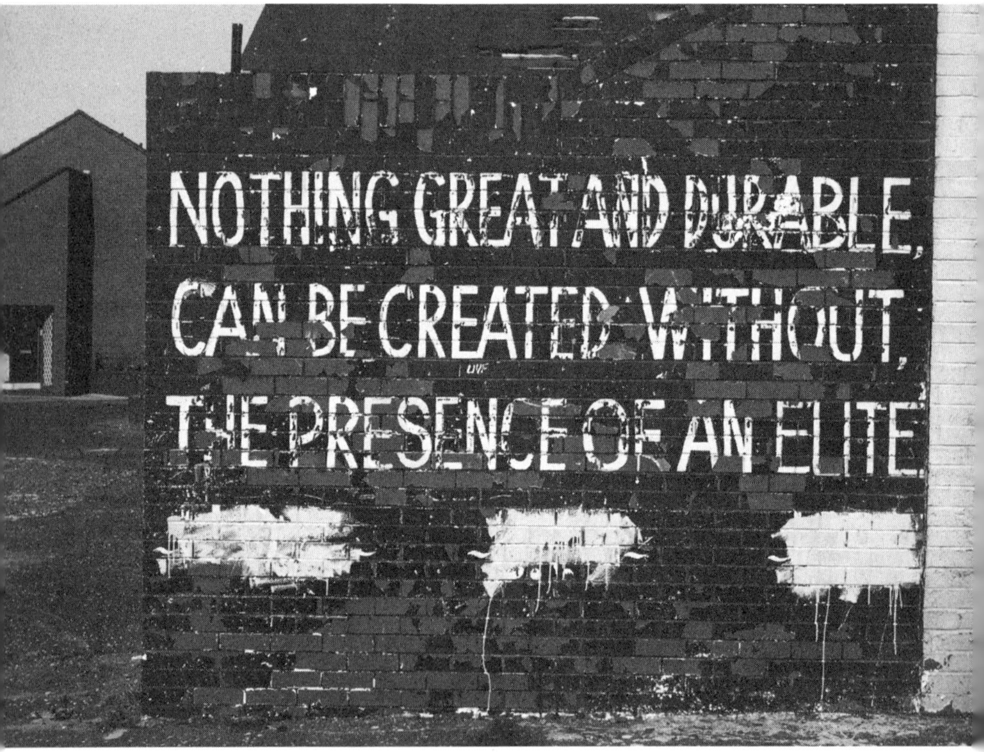
NOTHING GREAT AND DURABLE,
CAN BE CREATED WITHOUT,
THE PRESENCE OF AN ELITE.

The Strike (Thursday, 18 January 2024)

It's been cold all week, with last night the coldest yet, according to the early-morning weather forecast. A bit after eight I went out to open the coop and let the hens out. In every direction everything was coated with a crust of white; underfoot, the grass felt like wire and bounced slightly as I trod on my way. Amazingly, the coop's trap door was not frozen, though the rear flap, which gives access to the laying boxes, was. I waited and watched the hens as they slid down the gangplank and struck out towards their feed hopper. Usually they rush to their feed, but this morning they moved gingerly on the frozen ground.

We have a strike today in Northern Ireland: public sector workers (teachers, local government employees, health workers, train and bus drivers among others) are out. These workers have not received a pay uplift for two years, and their salaries are well below the salaries of those doing the same jobs elsewhere in the United Kingdom. The reason their pay hasn't increased and is lagging is that we don't have a government; without a government, pay increases can't be approved and disbursed. And the reason we don't have a government is because … drum roll … Stormont isn't sitting, and the reason Stormont isn't sitting is because … further drum roll … the DUP don't like the post-Brexit arrangements agreed by the UK government with the EU, which they claim, by putting a border in the Irish Sea, compromise the integrity of the Union and their place in the

United Kingdom … heavy strings, a slow largo. The DUP wanted Brexit and worked very hard to get the hard kind we ended up with, which makes one want to shout, 'Well, be careful what you wish for …'

Conor Murphy the Sinn Féin minister for finance for Northern Ireland, was interviewed about the strike on *The World at One* on BBC Radio 4. He opined the workers should be paid and it was wrong to punish them for a problem, a boycott by the DUP of government because of a sea border because of Brexit, blah blah, which was not of their doing. He sounded weary and lacklustre … But then who wouldn't be ground down by the mess and dysfunction of Northern Ireland … mess and dysfunction which, as was later confirmed, will run on (of course). Today was the final day the current crop of MLAs had to form an executive; according to the rules, if they failed to do it by today (to appoint a speaker and to form an executive) an election must be held within twelve weeks. But that won't be happening. As was explained on the news, legislation will be speedily passed at Westminster (it's amazing how quick the government can move when it must) to extend the deadline by which an executive must be established and thus there will be no need to hold an election until that new deadline runs out … Stormont will continue not to sit, government will continue not to happen, Heaton-Harris, Secretary of State for Northern Ireland, will continue not to release any money, the DUP will continue to bang on about the trade arrangements and, of course, the possibility for further extensions will continue to remain very much alive. So on the coldest day of the winter so far, when everywhere is frozen, our staying frozen politically for a further period has been set in train, thus confirming our status as the Kaliningrad of Western Europe, a product of old history cut off from new history, mouldering away on the edge of the United Kingdom.

★

In February 2024, devolved government in Northern Ireland was restored after a twenty-four-month hiatus following the decision by the DUP to re-enter Stormont.

Postscript

In December 1952 the Great Smog blanketed London. The fog was so thick it stopped trains, cars and public events. Having to breathe the noxious air killed 4,000 people, with a further 8,000 dying in the months following. In 1956 the Clean Air Act was enacted, partly in response to London's Great Smog of four years before. The act mandated movement toward smokeless fuels, especially in high-population 'smoke control areas', to reduce smoke pollution and sulphur dioxide from household fires. The act also sought to reduce the emission of gases, grit and dust from chimneys and smoke stacks. But the smogs continued. During the London fog of 2–5 December 1957, smoke and sulphur dioxide concentrations were similar to those in 1952, resulting in 800 to 1,000 deaths, and in 1962 another smog resulted in 750 deaths.

On 4 November 1958 I boarded a ferry in Dún Laoghaire, Dublin. I was four years old. With much belligerent clanging and growling – it was a very bad-tempered-sounding vessel – the ferry sailed through the night, carrying me and my mother and my brother across the Irish Sea. In the early-morning dark we disembarked at Holyhead in Wales by a swaying gangplank. As we walked to the station, the smell of oily steam enveloped us and the other half-awake foot passengers. When we found our train, we hurried on and into a compartment and settled down. Dry dust rose from the upholstery and my legs immediately itched. The light from the bulb overhead was watery, weak, dismal, the colour of old ivory (not that I knew what ivory was then). On the other side of the grimy window, out on the platform, were travellers in coats and hats, railway employees in uniform and carts loaded with great brown sacks bulging with mysterious contents, the names of English towns and cities printed on their sides – mailbags, as I'd one day discover. Everything I saw looked strange, spectral, unfamiliar, and nothing like Dublin, which was all I knew.

A whistle, shrill and inciting, followed by heaving, juddering and snorting as the train pulled away from the platform. The din of metal wheels running on metal rails. A mesmerising singing. The smell of coal smoke, exciting and exotic. Out in the country, as we gathered speed, a sense of power and brute force, heady, intoxicating, delirium-inducing. As we headed south and east, the sky lightened, and inside the train, especially on the windows, coal smuts appeared, lovely black tick-sized things. I squashed several and then smeared their innards of powdery soot around.

Sometime later, a railway station (Euston, though I didn't know its name then), enormous, echoing, reeking of tea; it appeared to be filled with a mist, which was in fact thin fog. Inside the fog, sounds were dampened, muffled; everything was unreal. Outside the station we caught a taxi, a London taxi, with slippery grooved seats – these had a peculiar leathery aroma – and a place by the driver (I'd never before seen anything like this) where our luggage was duly strapped in. The taxi took us through London: streets lined with vast buildings, pavements filled with pedestrians, roads clogged with traffic, and everywhere the fog again, thicker and denser than under the station canopy; there was nothing, it seemed, that it hadn't swallowed inside itself.

The taxi stopped outside 257 Cannon Hill Lane, a mock Tudor three-bed semi, with white pebble-dashed walls and a bow-shaped front window with diamond-shaped panes, one of a line of semis running from the bottom to the top of Cannon Hill Lane. On the other side of the road, however, instead of a mirroring row of houses, as I would have expected – in Garville Avenue, where we'd lived in Dublin, the houses were on *both* sides of the road – there was open ground. This was Cannon Hill Common, as I would soon discover it was called: acres of pale winter grass, lonely and wind-blown; oaks with bare branches, black and threatening against the sky; slippery grey asphalt paths, which were not to be trusted; and, in the distance, a brown wooden pavilion, sullen and uninviting. The fog was over everything, thick, dense, malevolent, and the whole scene was sunk in this medium it seemed, like a drowned world at the bottom of the sea.

It was Guy Fawkes, not that I knew what that was, and late afternoon, standing in our new home's suburban garden (dusty concrete paths, thorny roses with hard, glossy leaves, oozing fences stinking of creosote), as the light failed, as the darkness thickened, I watched rockets sailing across the smoggy London sky, extruding purple and green and orange and silver sparks as they flew, and then shuddering as they exploded, releasing silver and gold cascades of droplets; meantime, in the gardens of our neighbours, I heard bangers banging, Catherine wheels whizzing, sparklers sizzling and the accents of south London, never heard until now, guttural, forceful, choppy. The whole experience was magnified and intensified by the fog condensing and hardening about me (in the gathering dusk it had become yellowish-brown catarrhal stuff) and which, as I stood watching the fireworks, now slyly insinuated itself into my dicky lungs. It wasn't long before my bronchial tubes, irritated by the foul air, swelled in horror, which diminished their bore. But as the amount of air I needed was the same, I had to pull harder to get the same amount of air in, which in turn made my lungs' passages recoil still further and become even narrower. Pretty soon my face went red. I had to bend double and support myself with my hands on my knees. As I struggled to breathe, I felt light-headed, nauseous and panic-stricken. I thought I was suffocating, and the only feeling I could feel was a stabbing pain in the sternum and the only sound I could hear was my wheezing … This experience on my first night in London in the garden would be repeated ad nauseam over the following years, as the smogs, despite the legislation and our living in a 'smoke-controlled area', were a repeating thing.

Along with breathing difficulties came regular episodes of bronchitis – chest infections caused by irritation to the bronchi by the air. In order to prevent the bronchitis, I had to wear a bodice to keep my chest warm. It was believed (this was a medical opinion) that a warmer chest would be better able to resist infection. The bodice was a white number with pearl buttons and decorative borders and not a fit item for a boy. When we infants at Hillcross Primary did 'Music and Movement Stage One' (a BBC Radio schools programme which involved listening to a nice lady talking and then dancing around) we undressed and did the class in our underwear. When my fellow pupils saw me in the bodice, the boys (but not the girls – the girls didn't say anything) would hoot with laughter and shout the words they used for those who were physically defective. The bodice did have a feminine aura but, interestingly, this was never raised. In my schoolmates' eyes a bodice was in the same category as a hearing aid or a calliper or a crutch. It was a sign of deformity. Obviously, it followed, I hated the bodice. I tried to persuade my mother to let me wear a vest instead. A string vest even, like the tough boys wore, the tough boys whom I wished to emulate and who, of course, were the ones who shouted names at me. But this wasn't permitted. I was asthmatic and the bodice was an essential precaution. So the 'Music and Movement' ordeal ('Hey, look what Gébler is wearing …') was a fixture of my life then.

Another fixture were my visits to the doctor, always with my mother. The waiting room was always full of red-nosed, coughing, sneezing patients, all clearly sick and contagious. The doctor was Olympian, detached, kind but remote. His stethoscope's end was a freezing cold disc, which felt almost burning hot as he moved it around my bare back and listened to my roaring tubes. Afterwards, he would always write a prescription which, he assured my mother, would soothe and calm the pipes, thus ensuring their return to normal gauge, which in turn would mean normal breathing, no wheezing, no pain, no near-drowning experiences when I would bend double and fight for breath. A normal life, in other words.

From the doctor's surgery it was always on to the chemist's, a place of bizarre medicinal smells and long queues of more sick people (who also always seemed to be wet – it was always raining), to get the prescription filled, as people said, a phrase I never understood. My 'medicine' always came in great brown ribbed bottles. The bottle would be conveyed home with care, and within minutes of getting inside the door the cork would be pulled and a spoonful doled out into a spoon. The stuff was invariably the exact shade of pink as the gummy part of my grandparents' dentures, and once on the tongue, prior to swallowing, it would be registered as heavy, thick, viscous and stomach-churning. It would be swallowed with much grimacing and squealing. It wasn't nice but needs must, my mother and sometimes my father, who would sometimes come to see the administration of the medicine, would protest. And in the same spirit they would brush aside my objections to the bowl of ammonia that lived on the table beside my bed. The clear, foul-smelling liquid allegedly removed the invisible particles floating in the air that irritated my tubes and led in turn to the asthma attacks. That was the desired effect of the ammonia, but as far as I could tell its vinegary fumes did nothing but burn the wet tissues in my nose, at the back of my throat and down in my lungs and leave me feeling scoured, in the same way I felt scoured when I went into the damp toilets at school after Mr Woodcock, the boilerman and janitor, had washed the place down with water cloudy with Dettol and poured Jeyes Fluid into the sluices and drains.

The bodice, the medicines, the ammonia, not forgetting the gas fire that was sometimes kept going all night in my bedroom (I loved falling asleep to the fluttering, rasping noise the gas made as it burned and waking after a full night's sleep and hearing the very same fluttering noise as I had heard falling asleep), did not achieve what they were supposed to. Trips to the doctor, trips to the chemist's and long layovers when I would be confined to bed – sometimes for days, sometimes for weeks (I once was absent from school for so long that when I returned some children claimed not to remember me or to know me and in all seriousness asked me my name as if I really was someone they were meeting for the first time) – continued unabated and it became clear something would need to be done beyond what was being tried. I would need to go up the ladder (this was how the doctor put it), the medical ladder. I would need to go to the clinic. Tests would be carried out there and further interventions would follow.

We went to the clinic by foot, my mother and I. We sallied forth from our suburban semi, and instead of going right and down the hill to the doctor's surgery and the chemist's shop and the buses to Morden underground station, we went left and up the hill and into Raynes Park, where we traipsed along one suburban street after another until we arrived at a long, low white building with metal-framed windows.

We went through the entrance. Inside the atmosphere was light, airy. There were nurses in white, moving, gliding. The floors were wood, the benign and comforting smell of wood polish everywhere. There were tables and chairs in a waiting area. There were toys in a corner, a wooden train that ran on wooden rails – a glory – coloured blocks, a xylophone, a toy tool set and all manner of delights for a small boy. I was encouraged to play. I sat. I played. The weight of the toys, their colours and the freedom to gorge, to start with one toy and then move to the next, was intoxicating. While I played, my mother … actually, I don't know what she was doing, but at some point we left where we were and moved to a room, a consulting room, with an examination couch covered with rough sugar paper, a device for measuring height, a silver weighing scales, an eye chart and other paraphernalia associated with the practice of medicine, with all of which I was familiar from our GP's surgery.

I was examined and weighed and my chest was listened to. Then I bared an arm and turned the pulse side upwards and laid the arm down on the table at which I sat and someone – a nurse, a doctor – wielding a blunt needle, spotted the soft, thin skin of the underside of my forearm with different chemicals to which asthma sufferers typically reacted badly. Knowing which irritants provoked my asthma would help with the management of my condition. The groundwork done, I waited, and after a short while bumps appeared at certain places where the skin had been spotted. I was allergic, from what I remember, to house dust, blanket dust and horse dust among other things. A course of action involving avoiding these irritants was discussed. I remember no mention of smog and the part it might have played. And then a bottle, another brown ribbed number, appeared and its contents were decanted – but not onto a spoon, into a glass. It was also not pink but orange. I was invited to drink. It was a tonic and it would … I'm not exactly certain what it was supposed to do, but it would do something. I lifted the glass to my lips and drank, warily and then greedily because, oh my goodness, this was nothing like the foul pink medicine the colour of dentures; this was thick and sweet and delicious. It slipped down and left a magnificent aftertaste. At the time I had no notion of manna, but if I had had perhaps I would have used that word to describe this medicine.

There were further returns to the clinic, further tests, further examinations and further servings of the miraculous tonic. I have no sense of how long the clinic visits lasted, nor what was achieved, if anything. Little, I imagine, because in the years after I went to other clinics in other parts of London, where the same tests were performed and the same results adduced: I was allergic to house dust, blanket dust and horse dust among other things, and to control the asthma the best course was to avoid these things. The thing was, the asthma was never controlled. The hacking fits lasted all the way through childhood and into early adolescence, until one day I noticed something incredible, something I'd failed to notice: just like that, they'd stopped. It was a relief to be free of the asthma, which I'd regarded as a bane and seen as something that hobbled my life. It would be some years, even decades, before I understood the asthma had had a benign effect. For the weeks and months I'd spent in bed, there wasn't anything else to do but read. It had made me a reader.

In the house in Morden the thing in which I was most interested was the telly, which lived in the dining room with the black-and-white linoleum floor tiles and French doors that opened onto the veranda at the back. My father disapproved of almost everything that was shown on television, particularly 'American tripe' (cartoons and cowboy films especially, which of course were exactly the programmes I yearned to watch); he claimed such programmes rotted the brain as surely as sugar rotted the teeth and, just as he did with confectionery, he saved his children from decay by imposing a blanket prohibition. Our television was therefore almost never on (an occasion of permanent pain for me); the exceptions were either when something laudable and improving was showing – the news, a documentary or a Soviet film – or when something so big was going on in the world – for instance, when the A6 murderer, James Hanratty, was executed; when the Americans and the Russians nearly went to war over the siting of missiles in Cuba; or when President John F. Kennedy was assassinated in Dallas, Texas – that my father felt compelled to follow the coverage. At such times I would lurk by the dining-room door or in the kitchen by the serving hatch, which offered a direct eyeline, and watch, and in this way, I came to understand the world. There were two competing power blocks, the West and East, the capitalist and communist, and they were wary antagonists, each bent on lording it over the other, and in England, or Britain, where I now lived, there was a home-grown replication of this world model, with the Conservatives on one side and Labour on the other. As the understanding that politics was class-based seeped in, so did values and taboos: the Conservatives, I came to understand, were bad (very bad) and Labour were good (very good); voting Tory, I came to understand, was wrong, whereas voting Labour was right. These pieties went in deep, and became the foundations of my belief system.

By 1966, by which time I was twelve, my mother was living in Putney, at 87 Deodar Road, while my father remained in Morden. My brother and I shuttled between their houses. Thursdays were Putney nights, which was bliss, because on Thursdays *The Man from U.N.C.L.E.* and later *The Avengers* were on, both of which I was mad for (in Putney, unlike in Morden, I could watch what I wanted). On Thursday, 31 March 1966, there was a general election in the United Kingdom, which meant that on Friday, 1 April, when the results were reported, I was in Putney when I woke up.

My bedroom in 87 Deodar Road was on the ground floor in a room with a bay window overlooking the front garden. Early on that Friday morning I heard the jaunty footsteps of the paperboy as he walked up to our front door; then I heard the newspaper being slotted through the letter box, the flap clanging back once the paper was through and the muffle as it landed to the thick brown door mat. My mother had thrown a party the night before in honour of the local Labour MP, for whom she'd canvassed, so my interest in the election was already primed. As I heard the paperboy's footsteps receding as he clipped back across the garden towards the gate, I hopped out of bed and retrieved the paper from the mat. It was *The Times* of London, heavy, solid and smelling faintly of ink, a pungent, industrial odour.

I carried it back to my room, got back into bed and settled down. The front page was all classifieds so I had to go inside to discover what I wanted to find out – what happened in the election. The news was gratifying: the Labour Party under Harold Wilson had won a landslide victory – he had secured a huge majority. I read this and then moved on to the columnar sections detailing the constituency returns. And as I read, propped up against my pillows, my brother in the other bed sleeping still, transfixed, as I was, by the proper nouns, personal and topographical, of incredible peculiarity and variety, and the numerical information of mind-boggling exactitude, I enjoyed, for the first time in my life, the pleasure of political triumph by association.

During adolescence, when word streams started appearing in my head, I'd scribble the words down. It was the first writing driven by inner impulse I produced. Initially sporadic, the scribbling grew, in time, to became habitual. I called what I wrote 'diaries' because I'd heard of Samuel Pepys in English class and he kept diaries and I liked the idea I was doing that too. But of course they weren't exactly diaries, though I only came on the word 'journal' much later.

In those days the notebooks I used to record my thoughts all bulged like accordions because I was forever writing extra stuff I'd forgotten on loose sheets, which I then had to staple in. My handwriting was also terrible. Why couldn't I have a line of neatly filled notebooks on the shelf, like I imagined Pepys and other proper writers had? (I was an absolute booby who knew nothing, obviously.) I must learn to type, I decided. I enrolled on a touch-typing course.

The venue was a cinema on the Tottenham Court Road in London. Shortly before nine on the first Monday, I and the other trainees (all female) pushed through the cinema's swing doors and climbed the splendid wide staircase to the upper foyer. Here registration was undertaken and the fee paid. Then we filed through to the front circle where there were tables with manual typewriters attached by chains, with clean sheets of typing paper in shallow boxes at the sides. As I settled into a seat I smelt the ubiquitous cinema auditorium odour, a mix of velvet dust, stale tobacco smoke, Kia-Ora orange juice and the mysterious other smell that lingered in every cinema, which was the smell of the illicit, and even though I knew I wouldn't be seeing a film, I felt as if I was about to see a film.

At 9 a.m., the one dubbed the typing mistress by the class wags (she'd greeted us at registration) appeared before us. She was young and cheerful. She explained how we were to sit (straight back, forearms forward and flat, hands relaxed, fingers poised mid-keyboard); she explained the functions of the keys and the bars and the levers of the typewriter keyboard. She indicated the giant keyboard projected on the cinema screen. Whatever key lit up, that was the key we were to hit on the typewriter in front of us, but when we did *we were not to look down. We were never to look down.* That was the key. No looking down. Only looking up. Eyes forward at all times. Obviously, initially, we'd make mistakes. But if we persisted, we'd learn to find the key we wanted, instinctively and without thinking, and once we could do that, bingo, we'd be touch typists …

The auditorium lights dimmed, and in front of me, on the screen, keys and bars lit up one after the other, and I endeavoured to hit the same keys and bars one after the other on my typewriter, without looking down … My first sheet was a mess. My second sheet was not much better … but by the end of the course (it took a fortnight), just as the typing mistress had predicted, the system had worked its magic, and I could do it without thinking. I could go from a word in the head to a word on a page without looking. Amazing.

But though I'd learnt to type, I was also aware that my schoolboy brain wasn't like the brains of my clever schoolmates who could generate an answer to an essay question quickly and insouciantly. I needed to mull and to dream, sometimes for days, during which time, though I wasn't directly thinking about what I wanted to write, my brain would be working away. Eventually, I would know I could start and out would come the words; when I read them back they were always a surprise, and it was also always absolutely clear they could never have been created by an act of will. Given the way I generated language, I always performed poorly in exams.

In September 1970 I started my A levels. One was history. For the final examination I was expected to sit several exam papers but the board also offered candidates the opportunity to do a piece of independent research and to write this up in their own time as an essay and submit it. I liked this idea very much and decided I would do this.

At the time I was living in my mother's house in Chelsea, London. The house was in a three-sided square (the open fourth side bounded the King's Road). Most of the houses, including the one where I lived, were three storeys over a basement. They were built of yellow London brick, with stucco decorations on the corners, under the eaves, across the basement and the ground floor and around the pillars at the front. In the middle of the square there was a gated communal garden enclosed by black railings, with paths of yellow gravel, old trees, shrubberies and stretches of thin grass through which London's black soil showed through. I liked walking about the square – it was mostly empty, unpeopled and a good place to dream – and when I was walking around I would often conjure up images drawn from films like *The Railway Children* because to me it seemed this was the sort of space where such images of a Victorian and an Edwardian England belonged: thus, tramping about, I'd imagine little boys in boaters and tight jackets rolling hoops along the paths; girls in spotless pinafores, their long hair tied with ribbons, carrying their dolls and butterfly nets; nannies with little toques pinned to their tightly coiled hair, pushing heavy metal perambulators; moustachioed gallants in blazers and boaters; and lovely belles with parasols and veils, holding their skirts and clipping along in their button boots.

The houses in the square shared a look, but at the end furthest from the King's Road, by a little cut that ran down to Old Church Street, there was a house that looked very different. If the majority of the houses belonged in a Trollope novel, this confection belonged in a story by the brothers Grimm: it had turrets and oddly shaped windows and was bounded not by black railings but by a high brick wall, a convent wall, inset with mysterious-looking doors. I had the good fortune to visit, and inside I found this house was full of small oddly shaped rooms, which were exactly what I imagined the rooms in this house should be like. The householder, whom I'd been brought to meet, was small and birdlike. She was a widow, and in a fluting papery voice she narrated endless stories while swirling melting ice cubes in the glass she drank from. Once (for I was taken to see her several times) she mentioned that her little Gothic marvel had been the site of a sensational crime, an aggravated burglary – there had been a death and there had been a public hanging – and when I started thinking about my A-level project I remembered what she'd said. Perhaps this was what I could write about: the break-in and the murder in the house close to home; the hanging, I assumed, naively as it turned out, must have happened elsewhere.

I went around to the Chelsea Public Library to do some research. The library was a substantial red-brick building; it radiated comfort and solidity. Inside it had the library smell which I'd first encountered in the children's library in Morden, a heady, intoxicating mix of book dust, glue, paper and industrial ink, augmented with the smell of floor polish. There was also the intensely familiar library sound. Low voices, bordering on a whisper. Careful footsteps, which indicated that the walker was taking infinite care to set their feet down as lightly as they could manage. The faint thump of books being set on table tops and opened, or being closed and going back on the shelf. The gentle bang of index drawers closing. The scraping of chair legs and fountain pen lids coming off or going back on. This last sound had more click to it than the others. And finally, there was that special sound that came when reading and thinking and writing and pondering were underway. The sound of concentration.

I set to with my research. I checked the index cards. I found some works of local history. An old map or two. Cuttings. I read that in the early nineteenth century, slums lined the Thames on the north side between Battersea and Chelsea Bridge. In one building lived two Eastern Europeans. The records described them as Jews. In need of money and believing they would find it in abundance there, the two men took themselves to the unusual little Gothic house I had visited. They broke in. The householder was at home. A struggle. A death – the householder's. The two men plundered coins, silverware and a watch. If they'd only taken coins they might have gone undetected, but the silverware and the watch, once they had passed them to a third party, led the authorities straight back to them. The pair were arrested, tried and sentenced to hang. The gallows to do the business were constructed in front of the scene of the crime, which I hadn't anticipated (no doubt the authorities thought there was no better site to dispense justice than in front of the house where the offence was committed – the kind of that'll-teach-'em schtick that those in thrall to punishment adore).

Until this moment, I had associated the communal garden with boys in boaters, girls in spotless pinafores, nannies pushing perambulators, moustachioed gallants and lovely belles in button boots. Now a new set of images. The sources of these were hanging scenes in films and photographs I'd seen of lynchings in the American south; Orwell's description of a gallows and what happens at a hanging (information gleaned from reading his essay 'A Hanging'); and the press and media coverage of cases like the Hanratty case, from which I'd acquired a sense of the horror and squalor of a judicial killing. This new material I laid like a second negative over the original negative, which showed dreamy images from an English belle époque. The two sets being jammed together by virtue of their being particular to the same space was disturbing and terrifying but also revelatory. As I was coming to gather from the study of history, in life all sorts of everything was mixed up everywhere.

After the image rush and the mind swirl of seeing two different possibilities belonging to the same place, there came, in the Chelsea Public Library that lunchtime, a moment of clairvoyance. I glimpsed what lay ahead. I would write. I saw that. I knew it. Didn't know what or how. Only that I would. I also gleaned that I'd be involved in the study of story but, as with the promise that I'd make literature, detail was non-existent. None of this arrived in language, or as a picture, or as an idea, or even as a thought. It was a floaty, gauzy chimera, a throb from I knew not where. But I didn't doubt its veracity. I was going to make things with words … better known as writing. I was going to write. This was non-negotiable.

Back at school, I talked to my wonderful history teacher, Miss Whiting. She thought the crime-and-punishment story wasn't a bad idea, but she thought a much better one would be an essay on my great-uncle Michael Cleary, a member of the IRA in the Irish War of Independence, a supporter of the Treaty and a Free State army officer. I had access to his diaries and letters from the War of Independence, whereas I'd no such materials concerning the Chelsea story. My teacher's counsel prevailed. I wrote the essay about my great-uncle. This was my first experience of real writing.

After school and before university, I got a job at Shepperton Studios as the runner on the film of Simon Gray's play *Butley*, which Harold Pinter was directing. To get to Shepperton I took the train from Waterloo – it was about fifty minutes each way, so I'd plenty of reading time. Some years earlier, Terence Kilmartin, a family friend, the literary editor of the *Observer* and a Francophile, who was revising C. K. Scott Moncrieff's translation of Marcel Proust's *Remembrance of Things Past*, had explained to me very kindly, patiently but also forcefully, in the course of a walk in a forest somewhere in France, that this novel, *Remembrance of Things Past*, by this improbably named writer, Marcel Proust, was a great work of art, one of the greatest ever, and I ought to read it one day. Being an impressionable youth, and Terence Kilmartin being an impressive soldierly fellow, I remembered the conversation in the French forest about the great French novel before I started at Shepperton and decided I'd use my morning and evening train journeys to make good on the counsel I'd been given. I set to. I read *Swann's Way* and *Within a Budding Grove*. That's as far as I got. I liked what I read, but as I hadn't got to the end, I had no sense of how the whole cohered.

Sometime in 1990, during the first year in Northern Ireland, when we were still living in the flat at the top of Rossfad House, someone from the

BBC rang me up. He explained, in his nice BBC voice that the writer Sam McAughtry was making a radio series for BBC Northern Ireland (title: *Northern Counties*; subject: the six counties of Ulster) and he wanted to come and record with me for the Fermanagh programme, seeing as I and the family had relocated here. And that was an odd move, the voice continued, as typically the direction of travel was away from rather than *into* Northern Ireland; but there we were, I was that lovely thing – a maverick. I said yes – I was always going to say yes – but I said it with enthusiasm. Who doesn't love to be classed a rebel? Oh yes, I was chuffed.

The day of the interview John and Lois, Rossfad's owners, from whom we were renting our flat, offered their sitting room with its huge sash windows and astonishing views of falling ground, shimmering lake water and a great Irish sky filled with clouds like enormous balls of tulle. Sam McAughtry arrived round lunchtime – in person, physically compact, like a nut; in manner, fastidious, precise, genial, an old-fashioned gent – lugging a tape recorder and a box of microphones. In the room-with-a-view the brown recording tape was threaded into place, the 'On' switch was clicked, the reels began to turn, and the tape snaked through the steel blocks of the recording mechanism. My interlocutor asked his questions. I replied. The talk flowed.

Afterwards, as Sam McAughtry rewound his reel, he asked what I wanted to do artistically. Did I have a particular project for which I was looking for funding? Well, yes, I answered, I did as a matter of fact. I wanted to make a series of films about 'ordinary' rural life in Northern Ireland, focusing on Fermanagh. Such films, I added, would show non-Northern Ireland people what a complex place Northern Ireland was and, additionally, might interest people living in Northern Ireland by offering them something closer to the truth of where they lived than they were used to seeing on television. I even said something about such films fulfilling an important public service. Did I mention John Reith, first general manager of the British Broadcasting Corporation (he assumed the title in 1922), who is credited with establishing the tradition of independent public service broadcasting in the UK and who summarised the broadcaster's responsibility and duty memorably and pithily as being to 'inform, educate and entertain'? I fear I did. And then, mercifully, I came to my senses. I stopped.

'I'll tell you what I'll do,' said Mr McAughtry. 'At the end of the programme with your interview I'll tack on "Young man seeks to make set of films. Interested parties should get in touch," that sort of thing. And you never know – something might come of it.'

I thought this was a barmy idea, frankly, but who was I to quibble? 'Why not?' I said, though I was certain this message would never be heard. As it turned out, I was wrong.

A few days after the programme was broadcast, Maurna Crozier from the Community Relations Council phoned me. She'd heard the programme, she'd heard Mr McAughtry's tag, and she'd a little government money intended for the seeding of projects that would amplify perceptions of the complexity of life in Northern Ireland. This money nudged the BBC to support the project, and the series *Plain Tales from Northern Ireland* was made.

I stayed in touch with Maurna, and one day she asked if I was interested in going into HMP Maze (or Long Kesh as republicans called and still call it) and working with prisoners on their writing.

Yes, please, I said.

Of course, she added, I'd have to see loyalists and republicans.

No problem, I said. I was an equal opportunities kind of guy, after all.

An incredibly complicated vetting process followed. It's hard to remember pre-ceasefire life, but in those days, before the paramilitaries so kindly agreed to stop killing us, the Maze was a high-security jail with a formidable reputation on account of those it held, who were men sentenced to imprisonment on account of offences they'd committed during our hateful and squalid conflict. The government liked to call them criminals, but everyone knew what they actually were, which no amount of dicking about with the language could alter – what they actually were were men who wished to advance their political objectives through the use of violence, and that made them very different to the people one normally met in jail, the so-called ordinary, decent criminals, or ODCs. Furthermore, not only were they men who had been committed to advancing their cause through violence (this was what had got them into prison in the first place), but they were men who still believed – or mostly believed, even though they were incarcerated – in their cause and advancing their cause, including through violence. Prison, for the most part, hadn't softened their coughs, nor altered their ambitions and objectives one iota. Most were potentially active, had kept their values and objectives intact and enjoyed support systems outside the prison. Given all this the system, quite understandably, was bound to be nervous about an unsupervised civilian wafting about the wings. The authorities really didn't want any accidents; they really didn't want anyone smuggling stuff in or out, providing information or whatever.

In order to make certain of my probity and trustworthiness, which was the best guarantee that there would be no security breaches, two RUC inspectors twice interviewed me at home about my family background, going back as far as my great-grandparents. My great-uncle Michael who had been in the IRA didn't appear to worry them. A couple of years later, following a telephone call with someone from the Northern Ireland Office who asked me a further series of complicated, fiendish questions, I was granted security clearance and shortly after started teaching in the Maze prison. At the time, friends wondered if my English accent was a problem. It wasn't. The paramilitaries knew my seed and breed, as they say in Northern Ireland (it was actually staggering how much they knew), and because they knew what they knew, they knew I wasn't a threat. Later, when I worked with non-paramilitary prisoners, so-called ODCs, my accent again was not a problem, though for a different reason; as far as ODCs are concerned, you are either on their side or not on their side, and as they judged that I was on their side because I was a teacher teaching them, the fact that I sounded like a toff didn't matter a jot.

In the noughties, during a clear-out of her house in London, my mother found the essay I'd written at school about my great-uncle Captain Michael Cleary for my history A level and sent it to me. I looked it over and saw it wasn't very good; on the other hand, I also saw that by writing it I had taken my first steps along the route that I'd vaguely understood, in Chelsea Public Library, that I would be following, and which over the subsequent years I had followed.

In 2021, on a whim – it was during lockdown and I had time on my hands – I decided to spend an hour or two on the internet reading around Christa Wolf (1929–2011), the East German novelist and critic who, besides being a critic of the German Democratic Republic's oppressive system of government (and lauded for her dissidence), had also covertly co-operated with the internal East German intelligence service, the Stasi, providing information on fellow East Germans. Wolf's duplicity had come to light when her Stasi file emerged after the reunification of the two Germanies.

My internet browse told me little. Wolf, I learnt, was an unwilling informer: she didn't volunteer to spy on her fellow citizens; she was compelled. I also understood the Stasi weren't impressed with her; having 'recruited' her in 1959, they'd discarded Wolf by 1961 on account of what they termed her 'reticence', although this counted for naught when she was outed. Her Stasi dealings appalled many members of the old East German intelligentsia. Wolf, they said, had presented herself as a writer who told truth to power (and earned plaudits in the West for so doing), yet for two years, which she'd kept secret, she'd served that power. What was she thinking? Indeed, what *was* she thinking? I wanted to know. I saw she'd written *What Remains* (1990), the story of a day in the life of an unnamed East German woman whose apartment and occupational activities are openly watched by the Stasi, though I didn't imagine that would be much use to me on the subject of her forced collaboration, seeing as the novel was about a pure, as opposed to compromised, victim of the Stasi. The better bets, I thought, were *One Day a Year, 1960–2000* and *One Day a Year, 2001–2011*, being her accounts of 27 September each year.

The origin of these texts was as follows. In 1960 the Moscow newspaper *Izvestiya* extended to the writers of the world an invitation to, in Wolf's words, 'Describe, as exactly as possible, one day of that year, specifically the twenty-seventh of September. It was a revival of that undertaking "One Day in the World" that Maxim Gorky had begun in 1935, which had not lacked appeal, but was then not continued. So, I sat down and described my twenty-seventh of September of 1960.'[1]

And having written up 27 September 1960, Wolf kept going for the rest of her life, writing up every 27 September. She died in the middle of writing her 2011 entry. I ordered both books, second-hand; they came; I read them; they were pretty useless on the Stasi story (as I ought to have guessed), but in a completely different and unexpected way, they were invaluable, revolutionary and inciting. They gave me a book, this book.

In the essay 'Why I Write', George Orwell cites four reasons for writing: 'sheer egoism', 'aesthetic enthusiasm', 'historical impulse' and 'political purpose'; but it's the third (defined by Orwell as the 'desire to see things as they are, to find out true facts and store them up for

1 *One Day a Year, 1960–2000*, Christa Wolf. Translated from the German by Lowell A. Bangerter (New York, 2003), pp. 13–14.

the use of posterity')[2] that was the primary impulse, I thought, underpinning Wolf's *One Day a Year* books. Of course, historical impulse, in her hands, has two faces – the personal *and* the political – and using only moments (just what happened on or around 27 September each year) Wolf communicates her personal human story *and* the vast impersonal historical-cum-political story of her period, including the fall of the Berlin Wall, the disappearance of East Germany, the collapse of Yugoslavia, the implosion of the Balkans, the emergence of new Balkan states, the collapse of the Soviet Union, the terrible wars waged by the allies in Kuwait, Afghanistan and Iraq, the triumph of neo-liberalism and the ravaging and despoiling of the whole planet thanks to globalisation. Her shards might be small but with them Wolf contrived an epic, and when I saw that, I knew what to do with my own journals (proving again the late Cormac McCarthy was right when he asserted literature's dirty secret was that books really do indeed come out of books).

In 2022 I was invited to a conference, 'The Irish Proust'. I downloaded the whole of *Remembrance of Things Past* onto my phone, and for six or seven months I walked and listened, listened and walked. It all made a strong impression, but the part that made the strongest came at the end of the final volume, *Time Regained*. In this section, the narrator, Marcel, is invited by Gilbert, Prince de Guermantes, to attend an afternoon party in his new house on the Avenue du Bois. On his way there, the narrator has a number of revelations, including how he can escape the paralysis brought on by his knowing he is mortal. By the time he arrives at the Gilbert residence, a recital has begun in the room where refreshments will be served, and as orders have been given that the doors are to be kept shut until the

2 *The Collected Essays, Journalism and Letters of George Orwell, Vol. 1: An Age Like This, 1920–1940* (London, 1979).

performance is over, the butler shows him into a little sitting room used as a library to wait. What follows brings one of the book's central ideas to a conclusion – what the narrator will write and where it comes from.

The paralysing dragon of the narrator's mortality fixation has just been slain; so it only remains for the narrator to decide *what* his subject is. Standing in the library, it hits him – everything he needs for a work of literature is already in him in the form of his memories: 'I understood that they had come to me, in frivolous pleasures, in indolence, in tenderness, in unhappiness, and that I had stored them up without divining the purpose for which they were destined or even their continued existence …'

The narrator then draws the compositional and the organic, the literary and the botanical threads he's been running for three thousand pages into a beautiful and perfect bow. This stuff of memory, he thinks, 'formed a reserve which fulfilled the same function as the albumin lodged in the germ-cell of a plant, from which the cell starts to draw the nourishment which will transform it into a seed long before there is any outward sign that the embryo of a plant is developing …'

The marvel for the narrator (and this reader) is he no more knows what's happened (a book has grown within him, or to be precise, the seed that will make the book has grown within him) than anyone knows when they eat 'those grains that are human food, that the rich substances which they contain were made for the nourishment not of mankind but of the grain itself and have had first to nourish its seed and allow it ripen'.[3]

First, I processed this passage impersonally. The stuff from which we make literature is in us and it is laid down when we aren't noticing. It's

3 *Time Regained*, translated by C. K. Scott Moncrieff and Terence Kilmartin; and by Andreas Mayor (Chatto & Windus, London, 1981), pp. 935–6.

the life lived, which is all any writer ever had or has. The material fate gives, is all you get; the only choice you have is how you respond.

Then I went over the passage again, this time thinking personally. Out of my own experience but without my knowing had come the nourishment from which a seed was currently growing, a seed which would grow … what exactly this seed would grow into, this remained to be seen but it would become *something* … and this seed was already in the process of becoming …

Finally, I had one of those accelerated backwards-running reveries, when something is supplanted by what preceded and in turn is supplanted by what preceded it, and on and on it goes, back and back … I saw reading Proust for the conference, stumbling on Wolf's diaries, the years of prison teaching, the essay on my great-uncle for my history A level, the moment of prescience in the Chelsea Public Library, the typing school, the early diarising, the reading about Harold Wilson's 1966 victory in *The Times*, the covert watching of television news bulletins, the endless clinic visits and the relentless smogs were all part of the haphazard process by which nourishment was laid in, and right at the end, like the first and tiniest Matryoshka doll, was a boy lying perfectly still in a bedroom in Morden with his book, while the gas fire whispered and his bronchial tubes moaned.

★

The world isn't well and the soundtrack of its malaise, like the hum of a strip light on the blink or the rattle of a rusting air-conditioning plant, is always there and it grinds one down … But hearing birdsong at dawn, seeing the Irish sky and its glorious clouds, finding the dining table in the schoolhouse laid with a white cloth, its edges falling perpendicularly, a vase of pink roses gathered by my wife from the garden in the middle … for a moment, I can ignore the dismal cacophony.

Photographs

p. 252 gable end, Belfast
p. 256 pothole, Co. Fermanagh
p. 282 Carlo Gébler, road, Co. Fermanagh

Acknowledgements

I would like to thank Christine Breen for reading the manuscript at an early stage and steering me towards the personal and then reading it again at a late stage and advising me what could go, Maggie Brooks for reading the whole thing (twice), Fred Caulfield for the penal information he provided, Julian Evans for his interventions, Virginia Evans for her encouraging counsel, Martina Devlin for alerting me to what was missing, Diarmaid Ferriter for his steer on Seán MacBride, Claire Kilroy for suggesting 'Three Encounters with Mr Bertie Ahern', Maya Kulukundis for getting me to the Irish Proust, Philip St John for further guidance, Geray Sweeney for preparing the photographs for publication, Tom Walker for tracking down 'Horseman' and Niall Williams for his advice on the poems. All mistakes are my own.

Some material previously appeared in a very different form: the 1989 entry in the Workers' Educational Association magazine *The Spark* ('Tales from Germany', 1992); the 1991 entry in *Esquire*; the 1993 entry in the *Observer*; the 1994 entry in GQ, the *Irish Independent* and *Omnibus*; the 1998 entry in *Irish Pages*; the 1999 entry in *Fortnight* and *Christmas Memory*, a compilation book for Syrian child refugees through World Vision; the 2019 entry in *Southword*; the 2021 entry in *Plough Weekly*. A long extract of the finished text appeared in the *New Hibernia Review*.

The author is grateful to all these publications for permission to reprint the materials.

Index